Who am I & Why am I in TREATMENT?

Robert E. Longo
with
Laren Bays

Paths To Wellness ~ Book One
Getting Started

NEARI Press

Who Am I & Why Am I in Treatment

13th Printing 2001
14th Printing 2003
15th Printing 2004
16th Printing 2005
17th Printing 2006

Published by
NEARI Press
70 North Summer Street
Holyoke, MA 01040
413.540.0712

Distributed by
Whitman Distribution
10 Water Street
PO Box 1156
Lebanon, New Hampshire
03766
603.448.0037
800.353.3730

ISBN# 1-929657-01-3

Acknowledgments: The authors would like to thank the late *Fay Honey Knopp* who edited the first version of this workbook and had the vision to see how it would help the thousands of men and women who have read and benefitted from it. We are grateful for the shared perspectives of the "child lover" in a Texas state prison and "the rapist" in a Connecticut state prison that appear in the front of the workbook.

Advice To "Child Lovers"
From An Imprisoned "Boy Lover" Who Read This Workbook

You call yourself "boy lover," "big brother," or "mentor." In the case of young girls you are a teacher of worldly ways, lover and protector. You've occupied much of your life and thinking either in relationships with children or in pursuit of such relationships. You're convinced of your good and noble intentions, and you profess great love for children. You can cite many examples of things you've done for them and of the benefits they've derived.

When you begin treatment, or when you open this workbook, you will find words, phrases, or assumptions that you feel do not apply to you or to those children referred to as your "victims." You have always denied or rationalized those terms. To give treatment a fair chance requires that you become objective, possibly for the first time in your life. It requires honesty with yourself, your group, your therapist, or trusted friend. And, it requires a sincere desire to better your life.

Questions to ask ourselves: Have I ever felt guilty about sexual relations with a child? Is there a possibility that I have caused present or future emotional harm to a child? Have I ever used drugs, alcohol, pornography, or gifts to either arouse or coerce a child? Have I used love? Is it possible that love can be a form of coercion? Is it possible that, fearing the loss of my love, a child will do anything I ask of him or her? Has my love had strings attached? Have I never considered the possibility that children may not be prepared to comprehend or cope with my stronger emotions and demands? Have I justified the use of my experience and intellect in convincing a child to satisfy my sexual needs? Isn't it true that, between an immature child and an adult, the scales that weigh the give and take of a healthy loving relationship are way out of balance in favor of the adult? Might I be, in reality, motivated more by my own selfish sexual and emotional needs than by any unselfish love of children? Has my behavior caused pain in my life pain that I've blamed on the system, religion, politics, or the child? Am I unhappy right now?

If you can honestly answer yes to any of these questions, then treatment will benefit you. As you begin to gain personal growth you will find truth in many of those formerly offensive terms. It won't be quick or easy, but your reward will be worth the effort.

A "Child Lover" in the Texas Prison System

Letter From An Imprisoned Rapist Who Read This Workbook

Usually a man who has committed a sexual assault doesn't know who he really is. He lives in a world that is governed by distorted thought and behavior patterns. Abusing others becomes a way of life and survival for him. Even after years of being an active participant in a nonintensive sex- offender treatment program, I find the question: "Who am I and why am I in treatment?" thought provoking and very difficult to answer.

As I read this workbook, it highlighted the reality and waste of my own life, the years of incarceration for personal crimes against women, and the realization that I never knew who I was. I also realized that I am still struggling to gain a perspective into identifying who I have been, who I am now, and who I can yet be. This workbook provides men who have raped, or have the potential to rape, with the chance to begin the initial investigation into self in order to provide answers to the "who" question. With the workbook as a guide, a man can develop the thinking process necessary to make a determination to commit himself to treatment. It is very difficult to be motivated towards honest and complete commitment to treatment when you do not know what treatment you need or what can be done to change the behavior that has caused you to harm, so easily, other human beings without thought or feeling for them. This workbook can help a man who wants treatment. It brings the problems down to the level of understanding ourselves even if we are helpless to alter the course we have taken in the past.

Nearly 30 years ago, I recall being interviewed and evaluated by a psychologist in a reformatory where I was incarcerated for attempted rape (though I had already committed an earlier rape as a teenager). I was motivated to ask for help but had no knowledge of what was wrong with me. The psychologist confirmed a need for therapeutic intervention to prevent me from victimizing other women in the future. Of course, I never received that help and never really sought it either until many years later when I found myself in prison serving a life sentence. In light of the information presented in this workbook, it is clear to me that the psychologist did not have any more knowledge of my problems than I had. As I read this book, I realize that had treatment been available to me earlier in my life, I might have been able to prevent my violence and rage from victimizing many women.

Information and knowledge are prerequisites to the treatment process. They have to come first; ignorance only reinforces the lack of trust in others and in the treatment process. Without trust in others, rapists cannot change violent and destructive behavior. This workbook provides the information and knowledge needed to motivate a rapist to seek help, either in a specialized sex-offender treatment program in a prison, in the community, or in a personal self-help program. Without learning trust, sex offenders cannot benefit from treatment. This workbook provides offenders with the direction necessary to begin to learn trust, and opens wide the door to full and committed involvement in the treatment process. It provides hope where there is little encouragement to have hope.

A Rapist in the Connecticut Prison System

CONTENTS

INTRODUCTION

You are reading this workbook because you are either considering participating in a treatment program for sexual offenders, or you understand that you need to help yourself with your sexual problems. In either case you have made a good choice. Each year in America tens of thousands of individuals, like you, are charged with a sexual crime. Many more are never charged with a sexual crime but know in their hearts that they have problems in acting aggressive sexually. Whether you have been identified by the court as having sexual problems, know that you have sexual problems but have not been caught, or are concerned that you may have some sexual problems, the fact that you are reading this workbook is significant. It indicates that at some level you desire to heal the distress that inappropriate sexuality has caused in your life.

Many sexual offenders are arrested and charged with sexual crimes, many are in prison or jail, and some are on probation. No matter what your current situation, you are fortunate because you are beginning to think about *how* you can change your life. You are making the first step toward a brighter future. Working through the exercises in this workbook or starting in treatment with a sex-offender treatment program will give you a good basis for a healthy future.

This workbook is written to give you some guidance through the *first steps* in treatment. It outlines a very simple way to start working on a very complex problem. We hope that as you begin to read this you will look at your life and find the inspiration, hope and desire to change your life to a healthier one. The authors both work in the assessment and treatment of people with sexual problems who have caused harm to others. It is our experience that the best way of gaining help for problems with sexual deviancy is to work with an experienced therapist and *at least* one other individual. This other individual must be someone with whom you can talk about yourself and all aspects of your sexuality. One of the earliest steps down the path towards committing sexual crimes is keeping secrets. Hiding your thoughts and actions from your friends and family is a sure sign that you are on the wrong track and heading for trouble. As you go through the early steps of treatment it is essential that you learn to trust someone else. The authors have worked in state penitentiaries, state hospitals, and in community-based programs. Even under the most difficult of circumstances, everyone who wants to can find a friend to share feelings and thoughts with and to get feedback and support from. If you are in the ideal circumstance, where a sex-offender treatment program is available, you will find a number of men with similar problems with whom you can share.

"You are making the first step toward a brighter future."

We very much recommend that you join, if at all possible, a sex-offender treatment program. This is hard to do. Even if one is available, you may find a number of excuses to avoid committing yourself in this way. One excuse is that it is hard to talk to other men about past shameful behaviors. Another reason is that, if you are not in an institution, treatment is very expensive. A third reason is that, if you are in an institution, you may be creating more problems for yourself by disclosing your crime. All of these reasons (and many others) are used as excuses for avoiding treatment. Our attitude is that those who really want help, so that they do not spend their lives in prison, or creating victims, or causing more shame and embarrassment to friends and family, can get it. Getting help and being open to it when it comes, takes courage.

If you are in an institution, you know that many rumors circulate about mental health, counseling, and treatment programs. If you have heard stories about the uselessness of being in a sex-offender treatment program, consider the source. Was the man who spoke to you about the program successful in it or not? Those who do well in such programs, receive help and turn their lives around. They will speak positively about the experience even though they may admit that the program wasn't perfect and that treatment wasn't easy. Others who have not done well in a treatment program will sometimes lie about the experience in order to make themselves look good and the treatment program look bad. Keep in mind as you think about getting help that *this is your life*. You are responsible for what you do and what happens to you. You can, with help, take advantage of your opportunities. Don't let others talk you out of doing what you know is the best for you, or talk you into doing something you know is not right for you.

No matter where you are or what your condition is, you are trying to change your life for the better. The most helpful and fundamental step for you to take is to begin being honest. Who do you need to be honest with? First with yourself so you can be honest with others. What is the first thing to be honest about? About who you are and what you have really done in your life. Many sexual offenders lie about their crimes, deny doing them, minimize their role and are unwilling to take responsibility for their behavior. No one likes to experience shame, guilt, pain, fear, anger and other negative emotions, but running from them will lead you to lie and deny what you know that you have done. It is also the first step to committing a new crime. Hopefully, as you read this workbook you will understand that you must accept responsibility for your crime, recognize that you have a problem, and want help in order to change.

This workbook was written with you in mind. We hope that it will help you to better understand the evaluation and treatment process, and how you can get the most out of them. It will serve as an educational tool to give you guidance as you begin to examine your life. One way of looking at the process that you are entering is to imagine that you are taking a long trip. To be successful and reach your destination demands a great deal of preparation before you start. It requires acknowledging that you wish to travel, identifying your goal, gathering the resources that will be needed for your livelihood and for emergencies as you travel, and then, after your preparations are complete, taking the trip. The evaluation phase of treatment is the time to take on the first of these tasks. It gives you a chance to set your goals, look at the road map, and gain some skills that you can use over the years it will take to make your trip. [If you are in a treatment program it also gives the therapist a chance to evaluate you and your problems so that he/she can help you map out the best route.] During the evaluation process you will have many questions about the road ahead. The more you ask, the more you involve yourself, the better you will know what the road will be like ahead. If you are working with a therapist and interact honestly with him or her, he or she can better prepare you to avoid some of the deeper potholes. Professionals, who know you well, can help you plan your treatment so that you can be surer of reaching your goal.

The evaluation period is also a time to determine the source and strength of your motivation to reach your goals. You gain the most from your work when you have a desire to help yourself. Your motivation to change is probably the single major factor to your success in treatment. At times you will find your motivation wavering up and down, becoming very strong and then very weak. This is normal. Almost every individual who starts down the road to change his life for the better has thought about dropping out at one time or another. When you have to face yourself or begin trying to change old habits, it gets tough. That is the time that a lot of sex offenders feel like giving up. DON'T!! That time is the most critical for you to stay in treatment and face your problems. For example, if you decided to stop smoking, the easy part is to know your goal (a tobacco-free life) and what you need to do (don't buy cigarettes, don't carry matches, and so forth). It is not until you stop smoking that you get into difficulty. Giving up at that point makes all the effort that went into your preparation useless. It also makes all your friends believe you a little less when you say you will stop the next time. If you are like most sex offenders, you have given up on difficult projects for most of your life. Now you have a new opportunity. If you find yourself *weak, tired, frustrated or angry,* **DON'T GIVE UP!** Be determined to succeed. One way of keeping on towards your goal is to talk with someone who supports your dream of a healthy life and understands your fears and frustrations.

> ***"DON'T GIVE UP!***
> ***Be determined to succeed."***

Take your time and seriously think about your life and what it means to you. Don't cut yourself short by discounting this chance to help yourself. Don't make up convenient excuses in order to avoid looking at yourself. Even if you are not sure of what you want, you have nothing to lose by trying. Most importantly, be sure to give being in treatment a fair chance and your best effort. We wish you the best of luck.

Robert E. Longo
Laren Bays

NOTE: The authors recognize that sex offenders can be male or female. However, since the majority of individuals we treat are men, and in an effort to make the reading of this workbook easier, we have elected to refer to sex offenders as males.

CHAPTER ONE

Why Am I in Treatment?

Many sex offenders come to a treatment program with one big question and one big goal in mind. The major question is: "Why did I commit the crime I did?" The major goal is: "To make sure to get the help I need so that I never commit another sex crime again." Therapy can help you start to answer this question and will provide guidance for you to reach this goal. If you are not in a treatment program and have decided to read this workbook in order to help yourself, you have probably asked yourself similar questions and have similar goals.

Why Change?

There are many reasons that sexual offenders enter treatment and decide to change. For some, becoming involved in a treatment program is a question of curiosity: "I wonder what it is like in treatment." For others, entering a treatment program is a way to avoid being in prison. Many become involved in treatment because the parole board, a probation or parole officer, or the courts require them to do so. If you don't want to know why you did your crime and you don't want to change your behavior, then you are reading this for the wrong reasons. No matter what your reasons may be, if you have committed a sexual offense, we would still recommend that you take the time to read this workbook and participate in the evaluation process. You may find new reasons why you want and need treatment. If you are not in a treatment program and have decided to try to help yourself by reading this workbook, we suggest that you read the entire book and do the assignments. If you are doing this on your own, you may want to return to this workbook over and over again (both in the next few months and throughout your life) to improve your understanding.

We hope that your reason for reading this workbook is to help yourself so that you do not commit another sexual crime. But even if that is not your main motivation, give yourself, the program, and the workbook a chance. Take time to see if there is anything important that you're overlooking. It may be that you will discover for yourself why treatment is important. If after the evaluation period and reading this entire workbook, you still do not want to become involved in treatment, then spare yourself another failure and consider what other options are available to you.

What Can I Get Out of This?

This workbook will help you to begin to answer the question of why you committed your crime. It will also assist you in creating some realistic goals so that you are able to get the help you need. It is important for you to understand that you will have to work hard to make progress. This workbook cannot set goals or make progress for you. Just reading it is not enough. Plan on doing some hard work. So when you think about the question "Why did I do this?" and an answer doesn't come quickly, don't become frustrated. It may seem like one big question that is overwhelming, but in reality it is a series of questions that you can answer while in treatment. Of course, the answers to your questions will *not* come at once, nor will they come to you easily. Finding the answers to your questions will require effort on your part. If you feel comfortable admitting to others that you have a problem, are willing to *ask* for help or seek help on your own, and work hard, the answers will eventually come.

Don't evaluate your progress by comparing yourself to others. Be aware that everyone is different and everyone works at a different speed. This is okay. If you compare your progress to how you *think* others are doing, then you can make yourself feel like a failure when you are not.

If your motivation is good, then you are reading this workbook to help yourself. You have a set of problems to work on that are similar to those of other sex offenders. You also have a special set of problems that are different from those of other men, who are either in treatment with you, or who work alone using this book. You will design a treatment plan that meets all your special treatment needs. The plan must include: goals, both long and short term; methods to use to arrive at the goals; measures that you will use to evaluate progress; and rewards for achieving your goals.

It Is Necessary To Work Hard

The reason you are using this book is to reach your goals of personal change. If you remain as you are and don't understand why you committed your crimes, statistics, experience, and history indicate that you will more than likely go out and commit other crimes within six months or less. If you are honest you won't blame your criminal behavior on drinking or drugs, or on other people or situations. Most sex offenders say things like "I know I will never do this again," but there is no truth to their statements. Hope and willpower alone are not enough to stop you from reoffending. You must also have the tools and knowledge that treatment can offer you. Only then will you have the weapons you need in order to lead a responsible, nonoffending, and successful life. If you are not in a program and have decided to use this workbook as a self-help aid, then this workbook may temporarily serve as your treatment program.

Homework

At the end of each chapter you will find homework assignments. Doing these thoroughly will help you to gain insight into yourself and will make much of what we say more meaningful. After you complete each of the assignments, *keep them in a notebook*. You will be asked to review assignments and to get information from the earlier ones to use for later assignments. If you are in a treatment program, your therapist may only assign you certain of these homework assignments, or may give you assignments in addition to or in lieu of those in this workbook. If you are working with this book alone, we recommend that you do each of the assignments and go over them and share them with a friend who is supportive of your desire to help yourself. Again, keep all of the assignments you complete.

Sometimes you will need to go back and refer to an earlier assignment for one you are doing later on.

In summary, treatment isn't easy, but it can be a very rewarding experience. Some of these rewards are self- understanding, a better and more productive lifestyle, an improved ability to cope with life's stresses, and relief at being able to keep the promise to your-self that you will not abuse a new victim or harm the same victim another time. Changing your life takes hard work but it is your best insurance policy against committing future sex offenses. We hope that you will succeed in treatment and effectively change your lifestyle for the better. Once again, **good luck**, and let's begin!!

Chapter One Assignments

• Do Not Write In This Workbook •

1 In your notebook for homework assignments make three (3) columns. Label them #1, #2, and #3. Under Column #1 make a list of the good experiences you have had. Under Column #2 make a list of the bad experiences you have had. Under Column #3 make a list of experiences about which you may have felt both good and bad. The experiences you list should be as specific as possible. If the experience is one that happened many times, list a specific instance. For example: "My uncle sexually abused me. Beginning when I was six, he fondled me for three years." Or, "I did a lot of drugs. I experimented with different types of hallucinogens such as LSD and mescaline." This assignment will help you identify some of the problem areas for treatment.

Sample Work Sheet for Assignment #1

EXPERIENCES

Good	Bad	Good & Bad
Boy Scouts	Dad would hit Mom	Dad would be gone for long periods of time
Camping	Mom would yell at us kids	Parents fighting
Fishing with Dad	I would be punished	Leaving for school in the morning
Swimming in the pond	School	

2 This assignment will help you to look at your motives for wanting treatment-why you want treatment. The following is a partial list of some of the motivations of offenders who want to help themselves. In your notebook, make a list of your motivations for being in treatment. If you are honest with yourself, you will have both good and bad motives.

✓ I don't like being in jail or prison.

✓ I don't like how I have been.

✓ I don't like my sexual deviancy.

✓ I have seldom pleased my wife or family.

✓ I have lost a number of jobs.

✓ I have lost my family.

✓ I have wasted years of my life.

✓ I have hurt many people.

✓ I have never failed so badly as now.

3 Your motives for being in treatment are closely related to your treatment goals. A treatment goal is what you wish to achieve (in the future) while in treatment. A motive is what (in the past or present) makes you want a specific goal. For this assignment review Assignment #2 and begin listing your treatment goals. Your goals can be small or large, immediate or long-term. Examples of goals are:

✓ I want to control my abusive sexual fantasies.

✓ I want to learn to feel comfortable around other adults.

✓ I want to learn to communicate better with family and friends.

✓ I want to become more assertive.

✓ I want to improve my self-image.

When you have finished your list, rank your goals by number (with your first goal being #1) and place the ranking numbers on the left side of each goal on your list.

Review your answers to these assignments with your therapist and your group. If you are working on your own, share your answers with a friend or person you trust.

CHAPTER TWO

Am I Different?

Each sex offender is a unique person. There are many ways you are different from other offenders, but, though you may not realize it, many of your problems are just like those of other offenders. You will also find that offenders who have problems like yours also have had childhoods that were much like yours. In fact, if you get to know other offenders well enough, you will find that they made similar decisions to yours about those childhood experiences.

One thing that you probably have in common with other sexual offenders is the tendency to simplify your past. It is typical to find offenders who remember only the good parts of their childhoods and the people in it. It is equally common to find men who reduce their first 18 years into a couple of words, like: "Horrible," "hell," or "unbearable." The truth is that sex offenders, like everyone else, have experienced both good and bad times in their lives. One of the first steps in analyzing who you are, is to reflect on the whole of your experience. Consider your past, incident by incident. Try to remember both the good, bad, easy and hard times without distortion. Some examples of your good or positive experiences may have been: the time you won an award, were a member of the best Little League baseball team in town, or had a fun- filled family vacation. Your typical bad experiences may have been when you were: sexually or physically abused by someone, rejected by people who were important to you, or getting into trouble with authorities. Believe it or not, you and other sexual offenders have probably had some life experiences that were almost identical. However, like others, you probably have not told anyone about the true details of your life, or found out what someone else's was like. This lack of communication results from isolating yourself or keeping away from others. Because you don't know anyone else well, whenever you think about your life (and especially the bad experiences in it) you probably ask yourself "Am I normal?" or "Am I different from others?"

The feeling that what you have gone through has made you different from everybody else is a common concern. It is especially true when people have experienced hard times in their childhoods. It is natural to wonder why things had to happen to you. One train of thought that you may have had as a young child is, "I must have deserved it, therefore I am a bad person. I'm different from others. I don't deserve a good life." The feeling that you are different can come from a variety of episodes in your life. One of the early steps in therapy is to find out if you are different or if you are normal. As you talk about your experiences and get to know the experiences of others, you will learn that what you thought were major problems or unique experiences that made you feel different from others are both common and solvable. If you are working on your own, you must trust what you read here and try to find another sexual offender with whom you can compare notes.

Common Bad Experiences

Speaking openly about these incidents in your life will help you identify problem areas for you to work on while in treatment. It will also allow you to start to receive feedback and help from others. If you had a traumatic childhood, it is important that you remember and share the "bad" experiences in your past. Bringing them out in the open is the first step towards releasing their hold over you. The following is a list of some common bad experiences and problems many sex offenders talk about:

1. "I was physically abused."
2. "I was constantly put down by my parents."
3. "I was sexually abused."
4. "I had parents who were alcoholics."
5. "I was the 'black sheep' of my family."
6. "I never did very well in school."
7. "I don't have a lot of friends."
8. "I had severe problems with my parents."
9. "I had problems with my brothers or sisters."
10. "I feel rejected by others."
11. "I am a loner and want to be alone."
12. "I had/have problems meeting and dating girls."
13. "I have sexual problems."
14. "I acted out sexually with children and adults."
15. "I drank/drink a lot of alcohol."
16. "I had/have a problem with drugs."
17. "I dropped out of school."
18. "I have never really liked myself."
19. "I have trouble meeting people."
20. "I have set fires."
21. "I have tortured animals."
22. "I have had sex with animals."
23. "I don't communicate well with others."
24. "I had sexual problems when I was a teenager."
25. "I feel angry a good part of the time."
26. "I don't trust others."
27. "I usually try to hide or ignore my feelings."
28. "I have had a hard time asking for help."

The list could go on and on. How many of the above problems have you had? How many times have you thought about getting help for your problems? How many times have you turned help away?

What Happens When I Don't Talk About My Life?

Most sex offenders have had many of these problems and others. The memory of them often contributes to your feeling uncomfortable about who you are. Also, because of your past difficulties interacting with people, you may not have learned much about intimacy or communications and as a result became a loner. You isolate and withdraw yourself from others. You may avoid being open and honest with people because you don't trust other people. Often you don't even trust yourself! This lack of trust often results from a history of problems such as those listed above, and because of your lack of trust you have never worked with anyone to resolve your problems. So, problems and predicaments you experienced as a child are like some of the problems that you still have today. For example, consider Gene:

> *Gene was a troubled boy.* His father, who was in the military, felt that strong discipline was very important. If Gene stepped one degree out of line, his father would have him stand in the corner rigidly at attention. While he stood there, his father would yell and scream at him "instructing" him in proper behavior. Gene learned never to answer back, other than to say, "Yes sir." If he answered other than with those words, then the drilling would often continue for hours. To escape this abuse, Gene tried to avoid any contact with his father. Because of this treatment and Gene's avoidance of it, he never learned how to talk out his problems appropriately. In fact, he never learned how to talk about any important matter with people at all. Now, as an adult, Gene still has the same tendencies. If confronted, he either immediately agrees, no matter what he feels, or he runs.
>
> You, like Gene, may have a backlog of unsolved problems in your life. Because of them, you may wonder, "Am I normal?" or "Am I different?".

Common Good Experiences

Everyone has had both good and bad experiences. Every experience influences your life. Good experiences, unlike bad experiences, don't cause unresolved problems in your life. Instead, they often lead to positive qualities in your personality and an optimistic attitude toward your life. Below is a partial list of positive qualities that offenders may have. You will find other sexual offenders who also have some positive qualities that are similar to yours.

✓ I communicate well with others.

✓ I am a good listener.

✓ I am smart.

✓ I am willing to help others.

✓ I am capable of learning.

✓ I care about others.

✓ I am good at my career/job.

✓ I am patient.

✓ I can make others happy.

✓ I get things done on time.

✓ I am creative in my thinking.

✓ I am good at sports.

✓ I am good at hobbies.

✓ I work well with my hands.

✓ I get to places on time.

✓ I enjoy helping others.

✓ I work at self-improvement.

✓ I am capable of changing myself.

✓ I can help myself when I have problems.

This list could be added to endlessly. Several of these qualities, or others like them, are also part of your personality. Sometimes, however, when you have a lot of problems, you may not feel good about yourself or recognize your abilities and strengths. You become overly concerned about how bad your problems are and overlook your good qualities. Learn to appreciate the good qualities as they are the keys to your recovery.

If My Experiences Are So Common, Why Am I Here?

Neither your past experiences nor your present problems make you abnormal. Your experiences and problems do not make you different from others. Rather, the way that you responded to your problems is what is not normal. Not using the positive personality qualities, resources, and strengths that were available to you was what was not normal. That you have committed a sex offense is not normal, and as a result of that type of behavior you are different from others who do not engage in similar abusive acts against people. Simply stated, committing a sex offense, a sex crime, or sexually abusing others is not normal. Therefore, you do have big problems and you must work to correct them.

Do you trust yourself? Do you trust others? If not, this is one of the first things you will need to learn in treatment. When you learn appropriate trust, then you can begin openly and honestly to talk about your problems and bad experiences. You will need to learn to build friendships, and being in treatment is the place to begin. When you are friends with the people you meet in treatment or others who are supportive of you, you can talk about problems together and arrive at healthy answers in a safe environment. You will discover that you are not unique or different from other men who have similar problems and have committed a sexual offense.

Together, you can help one another.

Chapter Two Assignments

• Do Not Write In This Workbook •

4 You have committed a sex offense. In some ways this makes you different from other men. Write down some ways you might be different than other men in society. Consider the following areas: sex, empathy, women, greed, lust, love, money, victims, anger, family, and children. Share your answers with your group or therapist.

5 Make a list of positive personality traits, qualities, or strengths that you have, for instance:

- ✓ I have patience.
- ✓ I'm a good listener.
- ✓ I like to help others.
- ✓ I'm good at working with my hands.
- ✓ I'm improving my health through diet and exercise.

6 Look over your answers to Assignment #5. Think about the positive parts of your personality and for each item you listed, ask yourself, "What effect does this have in my life?" Now write down some of the effects good qualities have. Some examples might be:

- ✓ I'm patient. When frustrating problems come, I can stay calm.
- ✓ I'm a good listener. When friends need to talk, they come to me.
- ✓ I like to help others. When a crisis happens, friends know I will help.
- ✓ I'm good at working with my hands. I can build anything out of wood.

Review your answers to these assignments with your therapist and your group. If you are working on your own, share your answers with a friend or person you trust.

CHAPTER THREE

What Is Evaluation?

The very first part of becoming involved in treatment is evaluation. If you are in a treatment program, during the evaluation period you will have a number of tasks. Exactly what you will be asked to do will depend upon the program you are in and its requirements. All treatment programs will be looking at your motivation and investment in getting well. If you are not in a treatment program, this workbook will guide you in the things you need to do. In Chapter Seven, "My Past, My Present, and My Future," you will read more about your unhealthy habits of wrong feeling, thought, and behavior. You can learn to change these old sick habits into healthier ones. To do so requires investment, responsibility, and accountability. This chapter will discuss how you can learn to think about these three qualities while you are in the evaluation process.

Investment

One very important aspect of being in evaluation is determining how invested you are in the treatment process. Whenever you want something in your life you have to be willing to make an investment, or put something of value in it. To invest is to make a commitment for a future benefit. It gives you an advantage in life. If you buy a home, you are making an investment (putting money) in your future. If you marry, you are making an investment in a life-long relationship. The purchase of tools or an education is an investment in your job or career.

Until now you have had an investment. That is, you have put your time and energy in deviant thinking and sexual aggression. For whatever reasons, you invested your time and energy in rape, child molestation, sexual aggression, sexual abuse, abusive sexual fantasies, or other destructive behaviors. You may never have thought of it that way in the past, but the fact that you have continued to have fantasies, expose yourself, or "peep" on others, make obscene phone calls, rape people, or molest children shows that you had an investment in what you were doing. Because you did not stop, report your behavior to the authorities, or go into treatment when you began to do these things, it is apparent that you were too invested in the behavior to give it up or stop it. Now you will need to make an equally strong investment of time and energy in order to change your behavior.

> *"If you are responsible, then it means you are reliable and trustworthy."*

Being in treatment requires that you make an investment in your self and your future. The strength of your investment is shown by your motivation to change. If you have a strong motivation and are invested, you will show it by your active participation in your treatment sessions. You will show it by a thorough completion of your homework assignments. You will show your investment by how you treat others. Do you help them in discussing treatment questions? Are you being supportive of their efforts? Do you confront them appropriately when they are being harmful to themselves, to others, or the program? Investment in yourself, your treatment, and your real needs is one part of the treatment.

Investment in others, helping and supporting them when they need it, is the second major part of the treatment. If you are truly invested in treatment, then you are being a mature and responsible adult. If you are working on your own, your investment has two parts. The easy part is completing this workbook and all of the assignments. The hard part is to use what you learn from the reading and assignments to help others.

Responsibility

Responsibility is the second major element of evaluation and treatment. If you are responsible, then it means you are reliable and trustworthy. When you are responsible, you can be counted on. Someone can give you a task and it will get done. No one else has to think about it. Responsible behavior is being able to meet your obligations without complaints or excuses. Responsible behavior is an important part of daily life and treatment. Taking responsibility for your behavior and actions by keeping your agreements and following through with your obligations is an important first step in treatment. If you are working on your own, you should still practice being responsible for your behavior (and being honest with yourself in the process).

The degree to which you are responsible is the degree to which your word counts. It is easy to be responsible for tasks or demands that you enjoy or that offer some large reward. It is sometimes very hard to do the right thing when there is no obvious reward. If you get tired or you change your mind and decide that you really don't want to do something that you have committed yourself to, then it is very hard to be responsible.

Being responsible means that people can count on you no matter how you feel. (Of course, if circumstances change drastically, then you are responsible to remake your agreements.) Responsibility is being honorable. Being responsible to others incorporates everything from honesty, trust, and support to keeping promises or holding others accountable for their actions. Your responsibility to others is especially important. It means not only being responsible for yourself, but also helping others. One of the ways you can be responsible to others is to help them to be responsible for their behaviors and actions. This often requires that you confront others when you see them doing something wrong or not being honest. If you are working alone and in prison, you will need to use your judgement as to when it is safe and appropriate to confront others. We recognize the difficulty of this task in a prison setting. Be aware and careful about your personal safety if you are in prison, even as you practice being responsible. Being responsible to others is a process of giving and taking as you will learn during the next few months.

Accountability

The third major component of success while in evaluation and treatment is accountability. Accountability means that you are answerable for your actions. Accountability goes hand-in-hand with responsibility. Once you have accepted responsibility for your actions, then you need to hold yourself accountable for what you do. This means that you will take the credit for your actions.

Being accountable for the good things you do is easy. Everyone likes to take credit for a job well done. It is fun when others recognize your accomplishments, reward you, or give you positive feedback. Being accountable for your actions when you are wrong is much more difficult and easy to avoid. No one likes to be the center of attention when they are called on the carpet, punished, or reprimanded for irresponsible behavior. While you are in evaluation and treatment, and in the future, you will need to be accountable for all your behaviors and decisions, whether they are right or wrong, good or bad, appropriate or inappropriate.

Part of being accountable is that you have to be able to explain your actions and the reasoning behind your behavior. If you have an investment in the program, in helping others, and in your progress, accountability is essential. If you are mature and responsible and do a good job at something, you are accountable for the good job you have done. If on the other hand something you do is irresponsible, accountability means that you have to account for why you were irresponsible and be willing to take the consequences. Accountability is almost like an insurance policy. When you hold yourself accountable for your actions, you are in effect insuring that, if there is a problem, you will correct it. Even if you are working on your own, you can still practice being accountable.

The following three elements are tightly woven together (see Figures 1 & 2). Just like a puzzle, each is a part or a piece that makes the whole. One element cannot work effectively without the other two in place. If you are responsible, you have investment in what you do. If you are responsible, people will depend on you and you will become accountable for what you do. If you make yourself accountable for what you do, then you have investment in it.

Just like a puzzle, most of your problems are interrelated. When put together, they result in your being the person you are.

Participation

One expression of your investment, responsibility, and accountability is your participation in treatment. If you are in a treatment program, you should participate in treatment activities such as your treatment planning, group therapy sessions, completing homework assignments, and learning and following any program rules. Earlier, we mentioned that motivation was an important part of being in evaluation and treatment. Participation in these processes is a means

Figure #2

I
N
V
RESPONSIBILITY
S
ACCOUNTABILITY
M
E
N
T

of demonstrating motivation. You can demonstrate your commitment to treatment and show your motivation through honest and consistent participation, giving and receiving feedback, and confrontations. Most importantly, you must work at honest and open self-disclosure. If you are not in a treatment program you can demonstrate your investment, responsibility, and accountability by how you practice them in your daily life. One concrete way is to work hard in this workbook.

If you are in a treatment program, an important way to show your investment, responsibility, and accountability is by how well you complete the other requirements of the program. Acceptance and honesty will demonstrate that you are motivated to bring these three important elements into your treatment program. The list below is a partial list of tasks which your program may ask of you during the evaluation phase.

1. Write a complete autobiography
2. Complete psychological tests
3. Define treatment goals
4. Give and receive feedback
5. Give and receive confrontations
6. Interact on a regular basis with peers and staff
7. Participate in your treatment planning
8. Set a time-line for your treatment goals

These are just a few of the many things that men like you can expect upon entering a treatment program for sex offenders. These tasks are often accomplished during the evaluation phase. How you complete your tasks is used to determine your sincerity in wanting to be in treatment. Treatment is the only way you are going to be able to change your life. Your motivation to change will determine how well you do in treatment. If you are in prison and not in a program, there may be a psychologist available to help you with some of the above tasks and interpret for you any testing that you may have done when you entered prison.

Chapter Three Assignments

• Do Not Write In This Workbook •

7 Below is a list of historical factors and problem areas that may influence your treatment goals. Go over this list and for your therapist write down in your notebook those items from the list below that you feel are problem areas for you. Add any additional factors or problem areas that apply to you and are not on this list. Give explanations and examples from your life to show why they are problems. If you are working alone, share this list with a friend and talk with your friend about why you see these as problem areas.

- ✓ Lack of trust
- ✓ Physical abuse
- ✓ Emotional abuse
- ✓ Mental (psychological) abuse
- ✓ Sexual abuse
- ✓ Neglect
- ✓ Parents who were alcoholic or substance abusers
- ✓ Being rejected by people important to you
- ✓ Poor self-concept
- ✓ Problems cooperating with authorities
- ✓ Dating problems
- ✓ Marital problems
- ✓ Relationship or friendship problems
- ✓ Poor school performance
- ✓ Poor job performance
- ✓ Sexual dysfunction or other problems
- ✓ Drug and/or alcohol abuse
- ✓ Isolated and withdrawn from others, loner lifestyle
- ✓ Poor social skills, poor communication
- ✓ Lack of assertiveness
- ✓ Juvenile delinquency
- ✓ Adult criminality
- ✓ Family problems
- ✓ Broken home, parents separated or divorced
- ✓ Fear/running from problems
- ✓ Anger, quick temper, or unexplained angers
- ✓ Emotional insulation, closed-off feelings
- ✓ Low self-esteem
- ✓ Feelings of inadequacy
- ✓ Behavioral problems
- ✓ Aggression
- ✓ Gender identity problems or sexual confusion

8 Make a list of ten strengths you have that you can use to work on the problem areas you listed in Assignment #7. Write out the way you feel each strength you listed can help you.

9 **Part 1:** In Chapter Three we talked about investment. Look at the list below and estimate how much time you invested in the following aspects of your crime:

- ✓ Planning your crimes
- ✓ Fantasy about your crimes
- ✓ Carrying out your crimes
- ✓ Regretting your crimes
- ✓ Finding a lawyer and talking with him or her
- ✓ Being in jail, court, and so forth
- ✓ Covering up your crimes

Now, multiply the number of hours invested in the above activities times the present minimum wage per hour (or the last wage you earned or present wage you are earning) to see into how much money your time translates.

[HOURS invested in crimes X money = MONEY you lost.]

Part 2: Estimate the amount of money you actually have spent in relationship to your crimes. Use the following list as a guideline for areas in which you may have spent money:

- ✓ Lost time from work
- ✓ Payoffs or gifts to victims
- ✓ Destroying evidence
- ✓ Moving to avoid detection
- ✓ Pornography, videos, and other adult entertainment
- ✓ Court evaluations
- ✓ Treatment sessions
- ✓ Legal fees
- ✓ Drugs and alcohol

Add the two totals from Parts I & 2 of this assignment. What is the final cost to you? How much time, energy, and/or money are you willing to invest now in order to get better and put your life in order?

Review your answers to these assignments with your therapist and your group. If you are working on your own, share your answers with a friend or person you trust.

CHAPTER FOUR

What Is Treatment?

An offender, who had been in several treatment programs, would drop out a few weeks after entering treatment. When he started his latest treatment program he asked, "Why did I fail when I was in treatment earlier?" This question is not an easy one to answer. The reasons for failing may vary from one person to the next. However, there are some similar patterns in most of those who fail in treatment. In order to understand why someone fails in treatment, it is important to understand what treatment is.

Treatment is a complex process of events and processes that includes at least the following parts. First, you have to recognize and accept your problem areas. Second, you have to recognize that sexual offending is destructive to your life and the lives of others. Third, you must develop a treatment plan so you know how to work to change your life. The treatment plan includes such tasks as identifying your deviant cycle, dealing with fear and anger, addressing issues such as denial and minimization, and a number of other issues and processes.

One thing is certain. Treatment becomes difficult at times. You, like the offender mentioned above, may find yourself wanting to stop when the work becomes difficult or psychologically distressing. When you experience this distress (which is associated with personal growth and change), you may find yourself being defensive. If you put yourself on the defensive, you will be working against treatment. The next diagram (Figure #3) may help explain this phenomenon.

Football?

Another way to view treatment is to compare it to a sport such as football. In football there are two teams. Your team, "The Saints" has two parts: a defensive team and an offensive team. Your opponents, "The Great Sloths" also have a defensive and offensive team. In treatment, your team The Saints are trying to score points over The Great Sloths. Your offense tries to score points for a better life, while your defense tries to block The Great Sloths from creating more chaos.

In treatment, both teams are part of you. The Great Sloths represent the "bad" parts of you that are afraid of being in treatment.

The bad part does not want you to change. It works against your "goal" of change to a

Figure #3

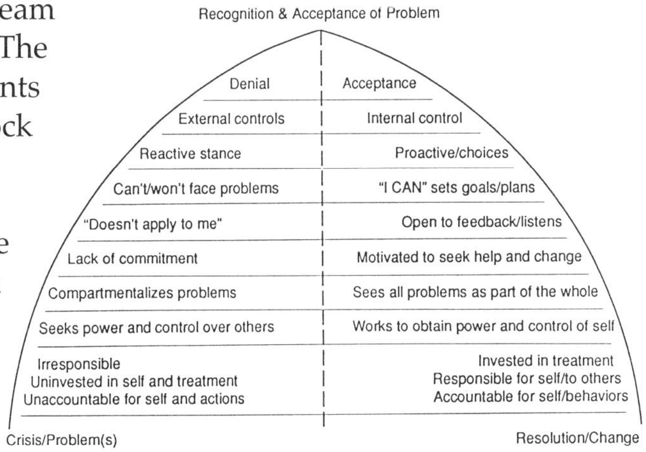

Recognition & Acceptance of Problem

Denial	Acceptance
External controls	Internal control
Reactive stance	Proactive/choices
Can't/won't face problems	"I CAN" sets goals/plans
"Doesn't apply to me"	Open to feedback/listens
Lack of commitment	Motivated to seek help and change
Compartmentalizes problems	Sees all problems as part of the whole
Seeks power and control over others	Works to obtain power and control of self
Irresponsible Uninvested in self and treatment Unaccountable for self and actions	Invested in treatment Responsible for self/to others Accountable for self/behaviors
Crisis/Problem(s)	Resolution/Change

healthier life. The Saints represent the "good" part of you that works toward reaching a "goal." In treatment the "good" offense is the part of you that wants to make changes, get better, and work towards the goal of self- improvement.

In Figure #3, the top of the diagram in the center is the "goal." Your goal means the solution to your problems. The "bad" parts of you work against your solving problems. The "good" parts of you work towards the goal of correcting the problem. The defenses that The Great Sloths use do not help you work on your problems. They block your effort to get treatment. The plays that The Saints use are the tools, behaviors, and ways of thinking that help you overcome your problems and make changes in your life.

Fear, anger, and depression are prominent feelings you will experience when you enter treatment. These feelings are used by the bad parts of you (The Great Sloths team) to block you from reaching your goals. You must be careful and constantly aware. Emotions of fear, anger, and depression will be used against you. There are many ways that you may be blocked from reaching your goals. You may turn your fears inward and be afraid of change. You may turn your anger outward and blame others for problems that you have caused. You may also be immobilized by depression. You may fear that those who in fact are trying to help you, are trying to harm you. If you are working alone, you may become afraid of practicing the skills introduced in this workbook. You may become depressed and feel there is no hope for you and stop working on your problems. Remember, these kinds of fears are common responses to making changes. The kind of anger that resents change is an old sick habit that must be fought against. The depression that you encounter will be one of the ways that you have used to stay stuck. To succeed in treatment, you will need to work long and hard to fight against these old patterns.

People have many crises and problems. In many cases they are afraid of their problems. At such times they become desperate and make vows to change their life for the better. Later their defenses come up and try to block them from reaching their goals. John is a classic example of such a person. His story involves drug treatment, but the story is just as true as if you changed it to "sex-offender treatment."

> John, the offender who failed in treatment mentioned in the first paragraph of this chapter, once almost died from a drug overdose. While he was still shaken and afraid, he promised that he would never do drugs again. John told himself he had to change his behavior and signed up for a treatment program. Eventually, when he knew he was going to live, he dropped out. He did not really want to stop doing drugs. For a brief period, his fear of dying and his anger at himself for getting into a dangerous situation worked to help him. Once the fear of dying diminished, the fear was transformed into fears of changing and of finding out that he had terrible problems. Later, his fear of change, fear of what others might think about him, fear of the unknown, and fear of giving up a past lifestyle shifted to anger. He directed the anger towards those who were trying to help him instead of directing it at himself and using it to help him become more determined to get well. He then dropped out of treatment.

Blocks to the Change Process

When first entering treatment, you may deny that you have major problems or minimize their severity. **DON'T DO IT!** Sometimes you are required to be in treatment by laws, rules, or regulations. If you react to these requirements with resentment, it will be harder for you to get much out of your program. You will be fighting treatment instead of participating in it. You might even see yourself as a victim of the "system." If you make excuses instead of facing your problem, then you are showing that you don't have a true commitment to help yourself. If you react with resentment, you are distorting life's events in your mind. This kind of distortion is probably similar to the kind of twisted thinking that led you to commit your sexual crime. The end result of such thinking is pain, destruction, and despair. If you are working on your own, the same sort of thoughts and feelings may emerge. You may become defensive, feel hopeless, and find excuses not to complete the workbook.

Compartmentalizing

You are most likely to feel overwhelmed when you look at the number and size of your problems. You may tell yourself that you have so many problems that you can't possibly deal with them all. You may begin to work on them separately, a few at a time, but eventually you will start to feel overwhelmed. This happens to most people who get into treatment. Seeing each problem as separate and not related to other problems is called compartmentalizing (COM-PART-MEN-TAL-I-ZING).

Compartmentalizing is the failure to see the relationship between your different problems. For example, you recognize that you have a drug abuse problem and marital problems, but think that they are not connected to your sexual deviance. If this type of thinking occurs, you are failing to see that your problems are interrelated. You do not have separate problems. Each of your problems is connected to the others. For example, if you have anger problems and drug problems, it would be foolish to think that the anger you experience doesn't effect your drug usage. If you are angry, you are more likely to try to avoid your angry feelings by using drugs. Or, if you use drugs, you may lose control and act out your anger in harmful ways.

You may use compartmentalized thinking to make your problems seem smaller than they really are. If you think that "I am a good husband," or "I am a good father," or "I am a good worker," and then think "Well, those areas of my life are fine, I only need help with my sexual problems," you are making a mistake. If you have violated someone through criminal sexuality, then you are probably not the good father, husband, or worker that you imagine yourself to be. The inappropriate thinking that took place before your crime also influences what kind of father, husband, or worker you are. So, as you become more aware of problems, try to see how each problem relates to the others.

Defense Mechanisms and Beyond

Denying, minimizing, rationalizing, and intellectualizing your problems are all defense mechanisms and are blocks against treatment (defense mechanisms will be discussed further in Chapter Ten). When you become defensive, you are unable to recognize your problems or the severity of them. As a result, you have a harder time accepting that you need help. When you don't accept that you need help, treatment cannot occur. If you are defensive and enter treatment, it is like paying for a new car and then refusing to drive it. When you don't accept your need for treatment, your involvement will be superficial and you also will be scared of being inadequate and will not trust anyone.

Once you have accepted that you have problems, understand that you need help, and begin to work through your defenses, healthy change is much more likely to occur. When you accept your problems and acknowledge that you want help, then you won't spend time fighting, but growing. At this point you will be actively involved in treatment. You will be able to change old patterns of thinking and behavior. So, a successful client doesn't react to treatment by being defensive, but rather interacts with treatment. He takes an active stance, realizes that he has choices, and that he can chose to change and become a better person if he wants to. He will practice engaging in new behaviors and develop strategies to change. This is the type of person who has learned to say and believe, "I can." He sets goals, develops a treatment plan, and works toward self-improvement.

> *"Each problem is very much related to all of the other problems."*

As you continue in treatment, you will become more open to feedback from others and will welcome input as to how to better yourself. You will listen to others instead of closing down to their feedback by saying things like, "That doesn't apply to me," or "I'm different." If you are working on your own, you will become more open with friends you trust. The motivation to change and be a part of the treatment program remains high, despite the fact that treatment at times is difficult and painful. You will come to realize that your problems are all a part of your self (the whole). Each problem is very much related to all of the other problems. Each problem is like a piece of a jigsaw puzzle. It is an essential part of your "whole" picture (remember Figure #1). As you solve one problem, you influence all your problems. After you work on many problems you will begin to have power and control over your own life. Then, instead of spending time and energy trying to overpower and control others, you can use your energy to succeed in productive activities.

Finally, as you work toward change and the resolution of problem areas, you will recognize the need to be sincere, open, and honest. As we said in Chapter Three, you are becoming more invested in yourself and the treatment process. You will understand the importance of being responsible for yourself while being responsible to others. In doing so you will become accountable for your behavior and realize that you determine your own fate.

It Isn't Easy

Because of your long history of being defensive, treatment isn't easy. Nonetheless, it is the best way you can effectively change for the better. Successful treatment also requires that you take a close look at your life and what you've done in the past. This process is difficult and often painful. No one likes to admit that they have problems and have hurt themselves and others. At the beginning of treatment, everyone feels this way. Later, when they see that others have similar problems and have felt the same way, it is easier to relax and participate. Your fears are probably just like those of the man next to you. When you are supported by your peers, your therapist, or friends, you can acknowledge problems and mistakes and work on changing them.

Treatment takes time. You may want to try to rush the process, but it simply won't work if you do. Many offenders come to treatment expecting the therapist to fix them or to do something to them to make them different and better, and to do it quickly and painlessly. They expect some type of magic pill. You may have similar expectations of this workbook if you are working alone. If time becomes a major issue, then the chances are good that you are an impulsive person who wants things now. Impulsive behavior is one of the factors that led to your being in treatment. Most sex offenders are impulsive people and that is a problem area that should be addressed as part of your treatment. Being in treatment is like being in college. You cannot receive an education in a few weeks. For some professionals it takes years of education to get their degree, and years of practice after graduation to become good at what they do. Being in treatment is much the same way. You may need to be in treatment for a year or more to gain any benefit from it. You must be prepared for times when you will know you are making progress, and for other times when you will feel like you are not making progress at all. Steady and consistent determination is the only way to succeed.

Cycles of Behavior

As you learn about yourself and your problems, you will discover that your problems are related to one another through a cycle of behaviors.

Jeff's problems are related to each other. One problem feeds the others, making them worse. Often these problems are tied together so that they form a cycle of behaviors for the individual. Jeff's cycle of behaviors may be described like this: (1) he feels his life is hopeless. This leads to (2) his feeling inadequate. This leads to (3) his not communicating or learning from others. This leads him to (4) feel like a victim. Feeling like a victim leads directly to (5) his anger and acting out. This leads to (6) his stuffing or hiding feelings of shame and guilt. This leads to (7) his feeling more worthless and having no self-esteem. This leads to (8) his avoiding people and feeling isolated and hopeless.

Treatment takes time.
You may want to try to rush the process, but it simply *won't* work if you do.

For example, consider Jeff:

> Jeff has a problem with anger. It usually begins with his feeling things are hopeless, that it is useless to try to change them. This makes him feel inadequate. He does not feel competent to solve problems, thus he is not assertive. The more inadequate and unassertive he is, the more he feels like a victim. This makes him angry and sometimes he explodes. Afterwards he feels shame and guilt but he stuffs these feelings and hides them, even from himself. His lack of assertion, his anger and stuffing make him feel worthless. Because of this he stays away from people and is a loner. His anger, emotional flatness, and lack of self-worth make him feel hopeless.

If we were to diagram Jeff's problems in the form of a cycle, the cycle might look like Figure #4 below:

Jeff's problems feed one another. He could break this cycle by changing the steps: If he wasn't so hopeless he wouldn't feel so inadequate / If he felt adequate he would feel more assertive / If he would be more assertive he would feel less like a victim / If he felt less like a victim he would not be as angry / If he wasn't as angry he wouldn't act out and wouldn't need to stuff his feelings / If he didn't stuff his feelings he would have better self-esteem / If he had better self-esteem he would have more friends and not be so alone. Together these make up a cycle of behavior and feelings. How does this way of looking at Jeff's problem compare with the jigsaw puzzle in Chapter Three, Figure 1?

Figure #4

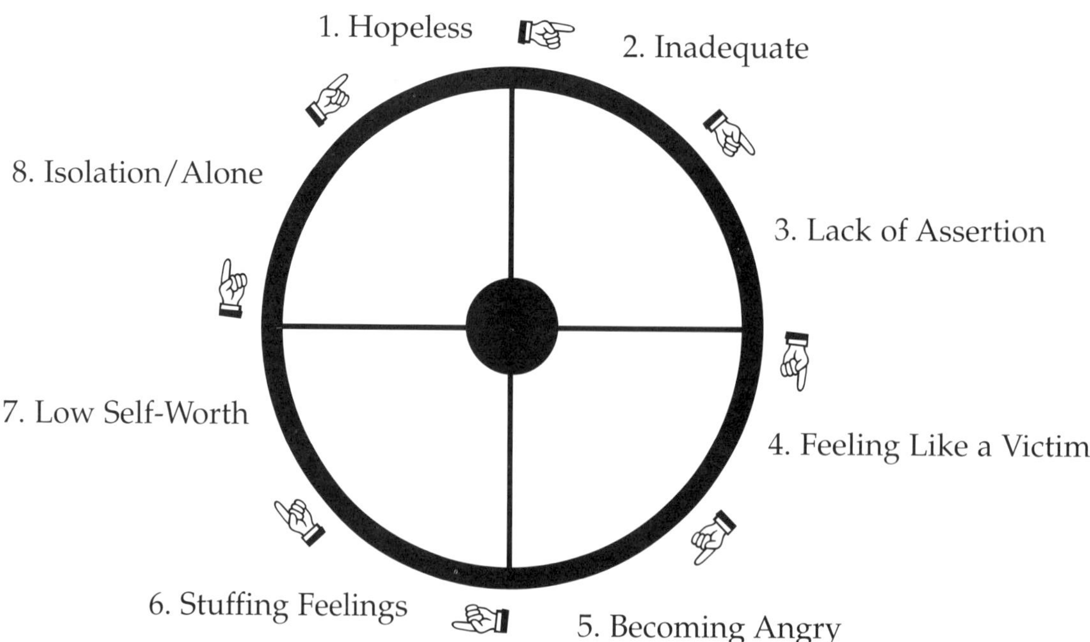

The Parts Make the Whole

A jig-saw puzzle is a complete picture that has many separate pieces. You too are a whole person made up of many different parts. Just as your problems are interrelated as we discussed in Chapter Three, they also are a part of you and contribute to what kind of person you are. When your problems are seen as part of a whole picture, that picture is the deviant cycle. When you are in treatment you are working to change the individual parts that make you the person you are. Because all of your problems are related to each other, as you work on them all you are actually changing your deviant cycle.

For example, if you have the same problems as Jeff, by learning to be more assertive, you would also learn to become a better communicator. Being assertive requires that you be able to communicate your feelings to others. If you can assert yourself and communicate your needs, you can express anger appropriately instead of stuffing it. As you can see from this example, thinking that you will work on one problem at a time (compartmentalizing) doesn't work. You must understand how all the parts fit together in your cycle so you can influence the whole cycle. In treatment, when you are working on improving yourself, at any given time you are working on a series of problems. These small problems (parts) combine to make your big problem (whole).

There is a lot more to the treatment process than we can tell you about in one brief chapter. You are gaining some idea of what treatment is about. Treatment is a process of identifying problem areas, setting goals for working on them, and developing a treatment plan (methods and strategies) as to how you will go about resolving your problems. As you proceed through the treatment process, your personal growth will be a painful experience at times. It is distressing because you will not like to admit to yourself and others that you have a problem that must be corrected. If you are working hard in a treatment program, these distressing periods are more tolerable. Through the help of your therapist, peers, and friends, you will be assisted and supported along the way. In time, you will begin to see light at the end of the tunnel and you will be less anxious about the unknown. As you make the necessary changes, you will begin to feel better about yourself which is a sign that you ARE making progress and getting better!

Chapter Four Assignments

• Do Not Write In This Workbook •

10 Based on the example given about Jeff, put together two different cycles that apply to yourself. These may be any behavior that you find yourself repeating. Two of the classic cycles that you may find valuable to identify are cycles of anger or deviant sexuality. Other cycles that you may consider are cycles of spending, gambling, alcohol use, depression, or super-optimism (being too optimistic or confident about situations or events in your life). Share your cycles with your therapist and your group. If you are working alone, share your cycles with your friend.

11 Does the cycle you just put together explain how you create problems for yourself? Does it explain how you defeat yourself before you reach your goals? Write out how each of your problems and goals is related to the cycle that you put together.

Review your answers to these assignments with your therapist and your group. If you are working on your own, share your answers with a friend or person you trust.

CHAPTER FIVE

How Do I Work On My Problems?

Once you have begun to look at your yourself, you will identify a variety of problems. Often the number and severity of these will be overwhelming. You may feel confused when you try to decide which are the most important ones. The first part of the solution to this difficulty is to get (and follow) the advice of your therapist. If you are working alone, read, think, and follow the advice of a good treatment manual. A professional is experienced in all the phases of treatment. He or she will know what some of the problems are that you will meet in treatment and can guide you so that you can successfully find your way through. If you find that you want to work on problems in a different order than your therapist, be patient. Your therapist is the professional. Do your best to trust the professional's advice. Professional advice can serve in the same way that a good field guide can. If you were going through unknown territory, you wouldn't trust your opinion about the direction, you would rely on whatever experienced advice you could get. If you are in a treatment program, then your therapist is a trained professional who knows that problems need to be worked on in a logical sequence for treatment to be most effective.

As you read through this workbook and do the exercises, you will identify many problems on which you will want to work. You have already begun this process and you will add to your list as you work through the manual. The next step will be to rank the problems you have identified.

Common Goals at the Beginning of Treatment

Therapists usually have three main goals for sexual offenders who have just entered group treatment. These goals must have a high priority, perhaps even the highest priority, because no therapy for sexual offenders can be successful unless these goals are reached. These goals are disclosure, feedback, and confrontation.

Disclosure

The first goal is to learn and practice open, honest disclosure. This means being able to openly and honestly discuss the details of your crimes, especially what you were thinking and feeling. You will need to share what you did before, during, and after your sexual crime. You will also need to discuss exactly what you did to your victim(s). These details may be embarrassing, humiliating, or shameful to discuss. Talking or writing about them is not easy, but it is essential if you are going to benefit from your work in treatment. Open and honest self-disclosure is the basic foundation of therapy. If you are actively working on yourself, then you will have lots of opportunities to test how honest you can be. If you are working alone, then disclose to a friend, or, at the very least, write out a true history of your life and crimes. Being honest with yourself is often the hardest work.

Feedback

The second goal is to learn to give and receive feedback. Again, if you are sincere in your desire to change, you will find many opportunities to receive feedback. A basic premise of treatment is that you can learn from others. When others who have similar problems are talking about their problems, you can listen and see parts of yourself in them. You can thus gain knowledge and information about how your behavior may have looked to others and also learn something about why you made some of your mistakes.

> *Getting close to people means being able to give and receive honest feedback.*

Direct feedback is when someone takes the time and interest in you to tell you how you are acting. This feedback is very valuable. It is also very scary. If you are open and really listening to what others have to say, you may hear how you really are, rather than how you imagine you are. Your fantasies of your behavior are often more pleasant than the truth. Getting close to people means being able to give and receive honest feedback. When you give another man feedback about how he is doing, he will usually respond and interact with you. Not only can you learn, but you begin to develop friends.

Confrontation

The third goal is to learn to appropriately confront others. Besides giving and receiving feedback, there will be times when you want to speak directly to others for being dishonest, holding back information, not sharing their feelings, allowing their personal desires to hinder the group's work, and so forth. Also, there will be times when they will want to confront you, especially if you are behaving in the same nonproductive way. This is an important part of treatment, and, if you are open to interacting with your treatment group in this way, you can learn a lot about how to live in an appropriately assertive manner. The lack of interaction is one of the limitations of working alone on your problems. Not only do you not learn about being appropriately assertive, but, if you're trying to work alone, you may think that you have made major progress or have even gotten rid of some of your big problems. This is seldom true. As soon as you begin to interact with others, you will find many problems that you thought you had resolved quickly resurfacing. Learning about confrontation is an essential early goal.

Disclosure, feedback, and confrontation are the first three goals. Other goals will be dependent on the program in which you are active.

A Variety of Methods

Another aspect of deciding which problem you will work on first is understanding what methods are available to help you. Without a method, it's difficult to work on a problem. For example, you may feel that you need to work on your relationship with your wife. If you are in prison and there is no appropriate setting for intimate conversation with her, you may have picked a high priority problem but discovered there is no method available to help you deal with it. You will need to find other methods.

There are a variety of methods used in treatment. Each of these has strengths and weaknesses. All can be valuable. If you want to help yourself with your problems, then at times you will be using each of the methods.

1. Reading for Understanding

You are now using this method. It can be important because it is a straightforward way that you can become familiar with information that is new to you. You can educate yourself about experiences or ideas that can give your personal life more meaning or understanding.

Reading can give you insight about your treatment, thus making you more aware of what needs to be done and how you can do it. Ideally, reading is a way of using others' experiences so that you can avoid some of the mistakes that are ahead of you. For example, this workbook is a group of readings that you have elected to read or that your therapist has assigned to you. If you go through it carefully, you can learn on your own about what you need to do, get a better idea of how to do it and avoid mistakes at the same time. Reading is so important that if you do not know how to read well, it is impossible to do much on your own. Only very specialized treatment programs can adequately provide treatment to individuals who cannot read well.

2. Written Assignments

You are also using this method as you follow the workbook's suggestions. Writing out assignments can help you to explore issues in greater depth and think them through more closely. Assignments can also help you to better understand information that you have read or heard. Clearly, to write anything meaningful, you must be familiar enough with the material so that it makes some sense to you. The process of writing requires that you organize it and think through the parts that are unclear. Often, you will hear or read something that you think that you understand, but only when you try to write it down do you realize that there were some important parts that you missed.

Some men don't like getting assignments that require writing. They complain that they never learned to write well, or that they can't spell, or that they have poor handwriting. To avoid what they consider "looking bad," they rush through the work as though they were trying to get an unpleasant task over with as quickly as possible. If you do avoid or rush through written assignments, you hurt yourself by not getting what you need out of treatment. Also, be aware that if you are in a treatment program, how thoroughly you complete assignments will be one of the ways that the staff will be able to evaluate your interest and involvement in the program. The staff will not grade you on spelling or penmanship. If you are working alone, then it is most important that you write out carefully and fully every assignment. Doing this will help you learn more and may be your only way of looking at your experience objectively.

3. Plans

Sometimes you need a very organized method to work on a problem. One way to do this is to make a plan (or technically, a behavioral contract). A good plan lays out how you will act when you encounter one of your common problems. For example, if you have a problem of being angry and dumping your feelings on others, you might decide to write out a plan that says that you agree to allow your peers to confront you whenever you express anger inappropriately. You might also plan to have them give you feedback when you avoid being angry and express yourself properly and effectively. You may even establish a reward that you give to yourself when you express anger appropriately for an entire week. This is an example of a simple plan. A good plan is often the most effective way of handling certain problems. It is highly organized, so that it makes it clear how to respond in a given situation, no matter how you are feeling. This is a real help when you are trying to learn to change behaviors.

4. Group Therapy

One of the firmly established ways of treating sexual offenders is group therapy. Group therapy is an important part of almost every treatment program in the United States. There is one good reason for it. It works! Group therapy involves meeting regularly with other men who have similar problems and working on common issues. A group is an excellent place to work on problems because it gives you a chance to receive feedback, be confronted, learn useful information, and watch other men effectively or ineffectively deal with their problems. It is also a time to learn to relate deeply and personally with your peers and therapists. Often this is the first time that many men learn to relate in a mature nonsexual way with other adults.

Sometimes your therapist will require that you present certain personal problems to your therapy group. This is a very common method for sex-offender groups to use. The group can then help you look at yourself "as others see you" and give you guidance when working on problems. Some men are uncomfortable with groups when they first enter them. This is a typical response, but with time you will begin to enjoy the group process and feel a part of this special group of people. Many men, who at first were scared of group therapy, tell us after graduation that the group is the part of therapy that they miss the most.

5. Individual Therapy

Many therapists like to conduct individual counseling sessions in addition to group therapy. Sometimes a therapist may see you individually for a short time before you join group therapy. The decision on whether you are treated individually will be between you and your therapist. There are many advantages to both individual (one-to-one discussion and counseling sessions) and group counseling. We feel that the use of both is the ideal method for treating sex offenders. We do not, however, recommended individual therapy without group therapy. Too often sexual offenders are able to play the "therapeutic game" while in individual therapy. Learning to relate to group members is often the way of enhancing your social skills as well as getting constant reminders from your equals about how you are doing.

6. Behavioral Rehearsal

Your therapist may give you specific exercises that require you to practice certain behaviors or rehearse thoughts in your mind. Some of these behavioral rehearsal activities are specifically designed to help you stop having deviant sexual thoughts and fantasies.

7. Classes

As mentioned in Chapter Two, most sex offenders have similar problems and backgrounds. One way to give information to them is to offer classes on specific areas that are common to sexual offenders. The program you are in may chose to offer classes, or have certain group time used as a class, to teach you about issues or social skills such as effective communication, assertiveness training, anger management, stress management, and other special topics. If you are working alone, you may find it useful to read books or take classes offered in the community or prison.

8. Aversive Conditioning

Most sex offenders have sexual fantasies about the types of crimes they commit. These deviant sexual fantasies are often exciting or pleasurable and usually occur with great intensity before a sexual offender commits a crime. Since these fantasies play such an important role in the commission of sexual offenses, the program you are in or your therapist may teach you aversive conditioning methods to help the fantasies be less pleasurable. If you do the aversive conditioning correctly, it also reduces the number and intensity of deviant fantasies.

9. Chemotherapy

Some sex offenders have compulsive fantasies that plague them for hours upon hours each day. When other methods to control these fantasies are not effective, several programs use Depo-Provera (also called MPA). This drug often helps offenders to better control their sexual fantasies and urges. Many men find that it is useful as a temporary adjunct to their therapy. Though it is considered relatively safe to use, it can produce side-effects with some clients and thus should be carefully monitored.

As you can see by the above examples, there are many tools that you can use to work on your problems if you are in a treatment program. The programs will also have a large number of specific techniques to add to the list. If you are working alone, reading and writing are probably the best resources that you have. Your ability and willingness to use these methods will help you and your therapist decide which problems you will work on first. In many programs, the first thing you will do is a lot of reading and discussion about your crimes and your life. Later, as you become more involved in the treatment program, you will use other techniques. Understanding the purpose of these methods will help you to feel more comfortable with the treatment process.

In summary, if you are in a treatment program only you, after discussion with your therapist, can determine which problems you will work on first. Your decision will also depend on the type of program you are in, the methods employed by the program or therapist, and the individual therapist's approach to treatment. If you are working alone, taking classes, reading, and writing about your problems will be the first tools that are readily available. Later you can devise ways to use these to help change your behavior.

By reading this workbook and completing your homework assignments, you have already begun to identify problem areas and techniques to resolve them.

Chapter Five Assignments

• Do Not Write In This Workbook •

12 Some of the most common problem areas for sex offenders to begin working on are listed below.

Self-disclosure	Giving & receiving feedback
Communication skills	Identifying defense mechanisms
Being honest	Giving & receiving confrontation
Sexual arousal control	Controlling fantasies

Make a new list of the problem areas you think you have from what you have learned about yourself thus far.

13 **1** Review your updated problem list in Assignment #12 above. Now make a list of short-term goals for yourself that you set in order to help you work on these problems. See the following example:

Long-Term Goal	Short-Term Goal
A. Talk about my problems with others.	A. Talk about my problems with at least one person each week.
B. Practice being honest.	B. When I lie or catch myself lying, I will stop the lie and tell the truth.

2 Now write out an action plan. This will include one or more methods that you will use to work on the top five problems on your list. This plan must be detailed and include:

(A) Why you chose the method

(B) How you think it will help the problem

Do this for each problem. You may need to get together with a friend to discuss your needs and plans. Be sure to be specific. Remember, identify one problem, think of the main method you may use, and suggest why and how that method will work for your problem.

3 Share your action plan with your group and therapist or a friend if you are working alone.

Review your answers to these assignments with your therapist and your group. If you are working on your own, share your answers with a friend or person you trust.

CHAPTER SIX

How Did I Become a Sex Offender?

"How did I become a sex offender?" Even if you have already asked yourself this question dozens of times, this is still one of the first questions you will ask yourself in treatment. Unfortunately you will find that there is no simple answer. You did not become a sex offender because you have a single problem. You, like most sex offenders, have often made poor choices and these poor choices have led to a variety of difficult life experiences and a multitude of serious problems. All of your history of decision-making, difficult experiences, and serious problems has been part of what has led up to your decision to commit sex crimes. (This long history is also why treatment takes so much time and is so difficult.)

To begin to understand the answer to, "Why did I commit a sexual offense?" will take you a lot of time, effort, and exploration. This is natural, for you have spent much of your life up to this point in thinking and acting in unhealthy ways. Therefore, you are not going to find the answers or change lifelong behavioral patterns in a few weeks. The assignments at the end of this chapter will help you begin to examine your background and feelings so that you can begin to find the answers about why you have committed a sexual offense.

Your History

The first step in answering the question "why" is to look openly and honestly at "what." "What" have you done during your life? Honestly facing yourself and remembering in detail "what" you have experienced and "what" you have done is one of the first steps in answering "why." Honestly remembering and fully disclosing (talking to others about) your sexual history is a good place to start. Most sex offenders have committed many sex offenses. They are afraid to admit responsibility for them because of shame, embarrassment, and concern about the consequences. Admitting the frequency of your criminal behaviors helps you overcome the tendency to minimize your problems and their severity. Also, it is a way of showing your genuine desire to get help.

While you are in treatment, you can talk about and discuss your other offenses. It is important that you don't give actual dates, times, places, and names unless you make a conscious decision to help your victims by reporting your crimes. While in treatment, no one can press additional charges against you with limited information. We mention this here because in order not to reoffend, it is important that you reveal your true sex-offending history. Only then can your therapist help you to form a complete and individually tailored treatment plan. If you are working alone, admitting your true history to yourself and your friend will serve the same purpose as open, honest disclosure to a treatment group.

There are a number of experiences in your life that are hard to speak about. For example, consider the number of sexual offenses in your history. Our experience with sex offenders, such as yourself, suggests that you have committed numerous sexual offenses. Very few sex offenders who come to treatment are here because they sexually assaulted only one person on one occasion. However, most offenders begin treatment with the intention of lying about the number of assaults they have committed. They often do this because they don't want to look bad or face up to the truth. But, lying to your therapist about previous sex crimes is like going to the doctor and lying about which part of your body doesn't feel good. If you have heart problems and tell the doctor you have a stomach ache, he cannot diagnose the problem properly and give you the best medicine. You put your life in danger as a result of dishonesty. If you lie about your background to your therapist, he or she cannot effectively help you do well in treatment. When you don't do well in therapy, then you raise your risk of reoffending and having future trouble with the law. As we stated earlier, treatment works best when you are open, honest, and willing to disclose information about yourself. Working alone with this workbook is no different. Don't lie to yourself or your friend. You must be open and honest with your friends if you expect to grow and change.

You must be willing to discuss any part of your life and sexual crimes. When you first begin to explore yourself, you do not know what is important. In fact, you may find that those areas of your life that you have the hardest time speaking of are the most important points to help you answer the question, "Why am I a sexual offender?"

Don't be hesitant about talking to your therapist. He or she probably knows more about your background than you think. Your therapist may have seen many hundreds of offenders and has learned to recognize the common patterns of experiences that are in many offenders' histories. These common patterns often are part of the process that led you to decide to commit a sexual crime. Even those close to you, like family and friends, have probably discovered patterns of behavior you engage in, especially when you are about to commit an offense.

Many, Many Problems

In the following problems we will discuss some of the common patterns in the lives of many sexual offenders. Much of this description may apply to your life. As you read, think about your history and see what is important for you. Thinking carefully about what applies to you as you read will give you a start on how to speak effectively about your life.

If we had to make some educated guesses about who you are and what your life has been like (based on our experience), here is probably what we would say about you. First, you probably haven't had a normal life. You probably grew up in a family that consistently had big problems. It is likely that one or both of your parents drank too much alcohol or abused illegal drugs or both. Perhaps your parents had or still have marital problems and when you were growing up there were a lot of arguments and perhaps outright fights between them. Your parents were separated or divorced at least one time.

We would also suspect that you had problems relating to your parents and to any brothers and/or sisters you have as well. Your family was not close. You probably felt like the "black sheep" and were punished severely when you got into trouble, which was often.

It is unlikely that you did well in school. You were bored most of the time, were always looking for excitement, and did not do any homework. Your grades were poor and it is likely that you dropped out or barely finished high school. While in school, you probably had a variety of problems relating to your fellow students in a social way.

We find that between 30% - 60% of sex offenders were sexually abused on at least one occasion when they were children. That is, an adult either sexually touched you against your will or seduced you at a young age. In addition to the sexual abuse, you probably experienced some physical or emotional abuse as well. Research suggests that as many as 95% of sex offenders have been physically or emotionally abused or neglected.

Socially, we would predict that you didn't do well either. You had problems with dating, felt insecure, and as a result withdrew from others. If you are a rapist of adults, you lived a lifestyle of a "lone wolf," coming out only to party and use drugs. If you victimized children, you probably were very shy and timid or kept a very, very secret life. In any case, you probably have few, if any, close friends and the relationships you do have with people are probably superficial.

You began using drugs and alcohol at a relatively early age (12 or 13). You may have been in trouble because of substance abuse; you are probably either an alcoholic or are chemically dependent on one or more drugs. Over 60% of the sex offenders we treat have drug and alcohol addictions.

The Problems Continue

As an adult you have created the same type of emotional life that you experienced as a child. If you have been married, you have had marital problems that were severe enough to lead to divorce. You may have had several marriages. If you have not been married, your relationships have been emotionally distant and problematic. In either case, you don't have very many close friends.

You probably have had difficulty supporting a family. You probably have had an unstable work history, going from extremes of overwork to odd jobs or no work. You may not have any real marketable job skills. If you are incarcerated you probably do not know what you will do for a living when you get out.

You probably have been in trouble with the law. Your previous offenses may have been relatively minor (in comparison to committing a sexual offense), but may have ranged from such crimes as passing bad checks or drunk driving charges to more serious offenses such as burglary, robbery, breaking and entering, and assault.

Finally, without a doubt you have had sexual problems in your life. You began to engage in sexually abusive behaviors at least by your teenage years. Most sex offenders have a history of exhibitionism (exposing themselves to others sexually), voyeurism (sexual spying on others, "peeping Tom"), making obscene phone calls, and so forth. In addition, you probably committed your first rape or molested your first child victim in your teenage years. You may have begun to engage in these behaviors anywhere from 13-16 years of age, or younger. You currently do have severe sexual problems. Committing a sexual crime is evidence of your problem. You have probably questioned your sexuality at different times, feel sexually insecure and inadequate, and have experienced a variety of problems in your sexual performance and sexual lifestyle.

What Do the Problems Mean?

An individual, like you, who has a history of problems in his life, is usually a very unhappy person. You may think that all of the pain and frustration in your history is reason enough to explain why you have problems. As you understand the history of your problems, you have taken a step towards answering the question, "Why am I a sexual offender?". It is not the complete answer. In your case, your problem-filled background resulted in delinquent or aggressive behavior. But there are many other people who have similar backgrounds who sought and received help and corrected their problems before they ended up in trouble. There are still others who have lived with severe problems all their lives but have used their experiences to become warm and empathetic people.

Understanding your history is only the first step in a long process of finding out the answer to the question, "Why am I a sexual offender?". The answers to this question and the important next question, "How can I stop my deviant sexual behavior?" can only be found through your active participation in a specialized treatment program for sexual offenders. At the least, you can get a start on answering these questions by going through this workbook.

Chapter Six Assignments

• Do Not Write In This Workbook •

14 In your notebook make a list all of the different sexual offenses you have committed. Include offenses such as exhibitionism, voyeurism, sex with animals, and obscene phone calls as well as rapes and child molestations. If you have attempted such crimes but did not complete them, please list them as well. Along side of each offense, write down how many times you did each type of offense and how old you were at that time. This assignment will be helpful to you in future treatment. Share this assignment with your friend, group, or therapist. The following list defines many different types of abusive sexual crimes and behaviors. [Note: Not all sexually abusive behaviors are crimes.] Use it to help you to make a complete history.

Different Types of Sexual Acts

Fetishism: A sexual interest in an object, like a bra.
*Voyeurism: "Peeping," sexual spying on others.
*Exhibitionism: Exposing your penis to others against their will.
*Frottage: Indecent liberties, "feeling someone up," sexual touching of or rubbing against persons against their will.
*Obscene phone calling: Making anonymous sexual phone calls.
*Zoophilia: Bestiality, having sex with animals.
Transvestism: Dressing up as the opposite sex for sexual pleasure.
Transsexualism: Desiring to become the opposite sex.
*Necrophilia: Sex with a dead person.
*Sexual Sadism: Gaining sexual pleasure by intentionally inflicting pain on another.
*Pedophilia: Desiring and having sexual contact with children.

Masochism: Gaining sexual excitement through suffering.
Other Types: There may be other types of sexuality than those mentioned. Some are coprophilia (use of feces for sexual excitement); urophilia (use of urine for sexal excitement); and klismophilia (use of enemas for sexual excitement).

** These sexual problems are also criminal acts.*

15

1 Write down the different types of fantasies, daydreams, or thoughts you have had about committing sex offenses or deviant sexual acts like those listed in assignment #14. For this exercise, do not write down the details of these crimes. Writing out the details is often an excuse for more deviant fantasies. Just list the type of fantasies that you have had. For example: "I have thought of raping women." "I have thought of breaking into a house to steal underwear." "I have thought of bondage."

2 Make sure that your list includes any sexual crime you have thought about doing but have never done. Write down the following about your fantasies:

A. The age you were when you first had them

B. What you thought and felt when you had them

C. How your fantasies affected you later, (did you feel guilty or excited; did you masturbate or hide; and so forth)

To assist you with this assignment, a partial list of feelings you may have had at times is listed below:

- ✓ empty
- ✓ mad
- ✓ excited
- ✓ relaxed
- ✓ weird
- ✓ confused
- ✓ high
- ✓ abandoned
- ✓ furious
- ✓ worried
- ✓ angry
- ✓ anxious
- ✓ sick
- ✓ glad
- ✓ concerned
- ✓ bad
- ✓ lonely
- ✓ insane
- ✓ afraid
- ✓ sad
- ✓ depressed
- ✓ elated
- ✓ foolish
- ✓ crazy
- ✓ good
- ✓ rejected
- ✓ terrified
- ✓ discouraged
- ✓ joyful
- ✓ happy
- ✓ bored
- ✓ stupid
- ✓ sexual
- ✓ nothing
- ✓ ugly

Review your answers to these assignments with your therapist and your group. If you are working on your own, share your answers with a friend or person you trust.

CHAPTER SEVEN

My Past, My Present, and My Future

Earlier you learned that you have problems much like other sexual offenders. You learned that this happened because sexual offenders have had common life experiences or have made many similar decisions. You also know that your personal problems are interrelated; one problem leads to and effects other problems. You also realize that problems are cyclic and there is value in working on them together, as one chain of events, instead of compartmentalizing them.

Your problems, for the most part, probably began in your past when you were a child or during your developmental years when you were a teenager. At these times you began to learn to make decisions that led to your sexually deviant and criminal behaviors. These behaviors were learned by you and you made choice after choice in your life that led to your offense. You learned how to choose sexually abusive and criminal behaviors. The roots of some of these learned behaviors are in your past.

Childhood Abuse

One of the common experiences of many sexual offenders is the abuse they suffered as children. The abuse may have been physical, emotional, or sexual. It may have been pleasant yet confusing (as when a teenage boy is introduced to sex by an older woman or man), or very unpleasant (as when a child is beaten or raped).

Physical abuse or neglect is defined as: a variety of injuries to a child caused by what the parents or protectors did or did not do. This definition includes failing to provide food, shelter, clothing, or medical care as well as overtly harming the child by beating, overworking, or excessively harmful discipline.

Sexual abuse is defined as: the involvement of dependent, sexually immature children or adolescents in sexual practices (1) that they either do not fully comprehend, (2) to which they are unable to give informed consent, or, (3) that violate the social taboos of family roles and/or the laws of the community. This definition includes such things as: incest in all its forms, involvement with underage prostitutes (in any country), or any other kind of sexual involvement with any child. An important part of the definition is "do not fully comprehend, or are unable to give informed consent." This means that children do not know enough about the consequences of sexual acts to be really able to choose to be sexually involved. For example, a child is offered a reward to perform a sexual act. All the child knows is that if he or she does this thing they will get a reward. What the child does not know is that they may get a disease, or that they may be forced to do the same thing again and again, or that they are being taught to prostitute themselves. Given these definitions, we find that many sexual offenders have themselves been abused.

The Past Does Not Control Your Present

This is not to say that you should blame your present problems on any part of your past. You can't blame your childhood, parents, other relatives, or your family's economic condition for committing your sexual crime. Blaming is a defense mechanism and not an explanation of why you made the choices that you did. You learned about defense mechanisms in Chapter Four and can review that chapter for more information about defense mechanisms (it will be discussed also in Chapter Ten). You can only hold yourself responsible for the problems and behaviors you have today. You are the one who did not seek the help you need, has not remembered how it felt to be abused, or has not learned to think about how not to let abuse happen again to anyone. However, when you were experiencing whatever hard times you had; that was when you began making choices that eventually led to your raping, molesting, or sexually abusing another human being. By the time that you did commit your sexual crime, you knew what you were doing was wrong and illegal. You certainly did not sexually abuse anyone in front of a police officer. So even though you are fully responsible for your choices in life, your past experiences probably interfered with your learning how to make mature decisions in your life.

A large percentage of people in the U.S. are abused in some way before they reach adulthood. For example, the best studies show that as many as one in five children will be sexually abused before reaching the age of 18. Given this percentage, imagining the number of children who experience any kind of abuse becomes overwhelming. While most people who are abused do NOT grow up to be criminals or sex offenders, most sex offenders have been abused as children. This abuse may have been of any sort or degree. It may have been neglect, physical, sexual, or emotional abuse. The abuse may have been primarily directed at you or it may have been secondary. If your parents were addicted to drugs or alcohol, then you were probably secondarily abused. When you were abused, neglected, or raised in an alcoholic family, you often had problems to solve. If you did not learn to solve these problems, then you may have used destructive behaviors or emotions to deal with them. The inappropriate use of these emotions will get worse over time unless you make an effort to change.

Past Abuse Influences The Present

Being abused has many effects. It can leave scars that last for years. Most of those abused feel ashamed about what has happened to them. Many victims are left with chronic fears and problems with unreasonable angers. Some survivors of abuse feel confused by a variety of emotions that they don't clearly understand and can't explain. Still other victims have learned to hide their feelings by pushing them way down inside so that they are numb. Common reactions to abuse include: guilt, denial, hatred, confusion, shame, embarrassment, numbness, as well as a host of other emotions.

When these feelings and emotions occur, either with great intensity or frequency, they can become fixed responses. These fixed responses are habits. Habits can be automatic ways of responding to different situations. Just as a smoker automatically picks up a cigarette, people with fixed emotions automatically pick up an emotion. These automatic emotions mean that one cannot respond appropriately to situations and an inappropriate response often causes more problems. Victims of abuse who have fixed emotional patterns must be helped to change how they relate to life by an experienced professional.

Often, if such people receive no help for their problems, they may begin to react to their lives through such behaviors as drug abuse, prostitution, relationship problems, low self-esteem, and/or aggression. The victims of your crimes, for example, are no different and are presently struggling with these problems and issues in their lives as you read this.

Often the confused and inappropriate emotions are reactions to the abuse. The antisocial behavior is frequently a way of coping with these feelings, and the thoughts which accompany them. Again, these inappropriate behaviors are practiced over and over and become ingrained habits. Later they will be supported by the belief system you establish around the behaviors. Here is an example.

George is a 30-year-old man. His parents beat him whenever they were drinking and got into a fight. He was very scared, hurt, and bewildered when his parents treated him like this. They told him they loved him and then would treat him horribly. He felt guilty and disgusted with himself. He felt that he must be doing something wrong to be treated like this. Gradually, he felt that his friends must also know that something was wrong with him. George felt ashamed and withdrew from his friends. As George withdrew, his friends noticed his withdrawal. They felt that trying to talk to him only disturbed and irritated him. So out of respect, they stopped bothering him and left him alone. George wasn't thinking too clearly. His emotions were confused. He thought that he was being rejected by them. He also began withdrawing from activities, thinking that he was not good enough to do well in them. After George had been withdrawn for a long time, he had no friends and no healthy activities left. He came to expect rejection or failure if he tried anything new. He also became afraid of people thinking that if they got to know him and knew what he was really like, they would hate him or laugh at him. He had no self-esteem and thought that he was a failure in life. He was depressed and lonely. When he was 16, he discovered that marijuana would make him feel better. He also found that when he was stoned he could talk with other drug users. He gradually began using more potent drugs and more of them. Then, in addition to his basic fear of people and lack of self-worth, he became addicted to drugs. He became increasingly fearful of people and authority. His life was nothing to look at so he didn't even trust himself any longer. Trust was completely gone out of his life and replaced by suspicion. After years of this pattern George was an angry, lonely, and frightened man whose life was a failure.

When George entered treatment he didn't realize that it was his current behavior that was now his biggest problem. When George was abused it started a cycle of behavior that George continued by setting himself up for failure and more feelings of rejection (see Figure #5). His pattern became self-destructive and each self-destructive act only made his problems worse. Because of his failures and confusion, he began to think about him-self as a victim. He became more powerless as he began to feel his fate was based on others' opinions or situations that others controlled.

Figure #5

ABUSE ☞ denial, fear, anger, etc. ☞ low self-esteem, feelings of inadequacy and insecurity ☞ withdrawal, loner. ☞ rejection. ☞ sees self as failure, a loser, unwanted by others or undesirable ☞ sets self up for further abuse, failure, or rejection.

Note: The symbol ☞ means leads to.

The example just given describes typical behaviors of abuse victims, including sexual offenders who were victims. If you were abused as a child, had alcoholic parents, or came from a family that was neglectful, you may have learned to respond to people in an unhealthy manner. You learned that because others' behaviors were not predictable (as alcoholic parents' behavior is not), they were to be feared and not trusted. As a result you do not assert yourself to get your needs met properly. When you don't get basic needs met in a healthy way, then you feel inferior. If you weren't abused, you may have learned to feel this way for other reasons. Fear, anger, rejection, distrust, low self- esteem, inadequacy, and other such emotions are treatment issues on which you will have to work.

You will find that even though you learned these behaviors in the past, they are all present and operating within you today. Your emotions, feelings, and thoughts directly affect who you are and how you act. Old habits of feeling, thinking , and acting help you to get caught in a cycle of low self-esteem and poor achievement. You will need to correct these old distorted feelings, thoughts, and emotions now so they don't continue to interfere with your new healthy life of the future.

Present Behavior Affects Future Behavior

There is an old and very true saying, "past behavior is the best predictor of future behavior." As much as you may not want to believe it, this is true for you and ALL sex offenders. If you have raped or molested people in the past, the chances of doing it again are very high. History and statistics have proven this to be true, and you are no different! There is one way for you to change your future, and that is to change your behaviors and thinking patterns through treatment.

So, as you begin to think about your past and work towards your future, stick with it. Don't let your past control your future. You are powerless over the past. You cannot change the past. You can control the future by how you allow yourself to feel, think, and behave NOW!

Chapter Seven Assignments

• Do Not Write In This Workbook •

16 Many sex offenders themselves have been the victims of sexual abuse or assault. If this has happened to you, write down:

1. The number of different types of abuse you experienced
2. The number of times that each type of abuse occurred
3. Your age at the time
4. The age and sex of the person(s) who abused you
5. Your relationship to the abuser(s)

17 Most sexual offenders have been victims of some type of abuse or neglect. Whether you have been physically, sexually, or emotionally abused, you have problems that resulted from the abuse. One of the ways of identifying the effects of your abuse is to remember how you felt as a child and what decisions you made about your life at that time.

Below is a list of traits or characteristics that are examples of common thoughts and feelings of abused children. In your notebook, make a list of all the items from this list and your own personal experience that you feel describe how you thought and felt as a child. Give an example for each.

- ✓ Blaming yourself for everything
- ✓ Rejecting compliments and praise
- ✓ Feeling different from the rest to the world
- ✓ Thinking "I'm not good enough"
- ✓ Thinking "Others are talking about me"
- ✓ Always suspicious, lack of trust
- ✓ Overly dependent on others
- ✓ Self pitying
- ✓ Experiencing guilt and shame without reason
- ✓ Thinking of yourself as a victim
- ✓ Feeling suicidal
- ✓ Only forming relationships with overly dependent people
- ✓ Difficulty forming good relationships
- ✓ Feeling angry a lot of the time
- ✓ Fearing people and situations inappropriately
- ✓ Feeling hurt by others most of the time
- ✓ Frequently feeling like you were going crazy or losing your mind
- ✓ Feeling lonely and empty inside
- ✓ Perfectionism — everything you do has to be perfect
- ✓ Fearing rejection, so avoiding even trying
- ✓ Not being assertive
- ✓ Couldn't talk about personal problems
- ✓ Lying when confronted
- ✓ Feeling controled by others
- ✓ Feeling depressed and sad a lot
- ✓ Coercing and threatening others in order to get your way
- ✓ Fearing any change
- ✓ Frequently frustrated with people and situations
- ✓ Compulsive behaviors
- ✓ Equating love with sex
- ✓ Abusing your parents or siblings
- ✓ Having no sense of humor
- ✓ Being unable to make decisions easily
- ✓ Covering up painful feelings with laughter
- ✓ Constantly having sexual problems

18 Take the list you just made from Assignment #17 and place an "X" by each thought or feeling that is also present in your adult life. Review the above list. In your notebook, make a separate list of the feelings that you DID NOT HAVE as a child or teen.

19 How do your thoughts, feelings, behaviors, and experiences relate to each other? Put your thoughts, feelings, and behaviors, etc. into a cycle that describes your sex-offending behavior. This cycle should be descriptive of at least one of your actual crimes.

Review your answers to these assignments with your therapist and your group. If you are working on your own, share your answers with a friend or person you trust.

CHAPTER EIGHT

What To Do If You Were Abused

What Is Abuse? Abuse is a major problem in our society, and it comes in many forms. For the purposes of this workbook, abuse means: acts or behaviors (including neglect) which result in physical, mental, or emotional harm. This definition includes unlawful sexual acts which may result in temporary or permanent emotional, psychological, or physical scarring. The most common forms of childhood abuse include beating or torture (physical abuse), overworking children (physical and emotional abuse), not providing adequate medical care, food or clothing (neglect), constant criticism or mental torture (mental abuse), improper exposure to sex either through sexual activity or by showing children sexual material (sexual abuse), and overdisciplining children (physical, emotional, mental abuse). All of these are simple examples of how children are abused.

Childhood abuse is violence towards children. It is often far worse than the street violence that one reads about in the paper. It is commonly secret, lasts for years, and affects the most defenseless part of our entire society. Abuse is a major problem in our society because the effects of abuse are very long lasting and recovery is very hard. If you were abused, this chapter will focus on some of the initial steps you can take to begin your recovery from your childhood abuse.

Abuse Is Not an Excuse

Sexual offenders often were abused as children. Of the clients who volunteer for treatment at state prisons, as many as 30-70% have been victims of sexual abuse and 95% have experienced one or more of the types of abuse mentioned above. Most of these people were reluctant to speak about their abuse for fear of not being believed, being made fun of, being viewed as weak or unmanly, and/or being rejected by others as a result of such disclosures. Often, it was not until they entered therapy and began to hear others telling about their histories of abuse that they started to understand the importance of acknowledging their abuse and began to speak about it.

Childhood abuse did not make you become a sexual offender. As you learn about childhood abuse, you will be tempted to blame your abuser for your current problems. Abuse in your background is only one of the many factors that has influenced you in making the choices that led to your becoming the person you are today. However, childhood abuse is an important area for you to understand. If you have read Chapter 7, you know that abuse creates long-term problems. You will have to overcome these in order to lead a healthy life. You can use the information and assignments in this workbook to help identify how you were affected by abuse. When you understand these effects, you will have a better understanding of the problems you need to solve. Discovering this information about yourself will help you to understand how your crime may have affected your victim.

Your Feelings Are Not Unique

At some time, all victims of abuse have similar feelings and reactions. The pain, hurt, and frustration that you have experienced are common to the majority of abuse victims. Your goal in recovery is to become a survivor who no longer allows past abuse experiences to control your present life.

Steps to Recovery

The first step in recovery is to acknowledge that what you experienced really happened. The second step is to learn to talk about your abuse and express your feelings to appropriate people. These two steps describe a simple way that you can face your abuse and at the same time learn that you are not alone. Talking about your abuse is a very important part of treatment. Like recovery from sexual problems, you will not recover from your abuse if you hide and ignore it. One way of bringing a hidden history of abuse out into the open is to talk about it. Talking openly with sympathetic friends will make it easier for you to identify the effects that abuse has had on you. Speaking about your abuse will bring to mind more details. As you speak, you may also experience painful and disturbing emotions, feelings, and memories. If these emotions occur, keep sharing by telling your friends how you feel. Sharing feelings, memories, frustration and pain with friends you can trust is one of the steps of your recovery. Sharing will not make distressing feelings disappear, but sharing might make them easier to bear.

If you are working alone, writing will be an appropriate substitute for talking. Writing out the history of your abuse and your reactions to it is a useful exercise. It allows you to see more clearly what may or may not have happened in the past. But, it is not as effective a way of working as having a friend you can share with. A friend can give you feedback, understanding, or ask pointed questions that can help you view your life more honestly. If you are working alone, it is useful to save your written work. Later, you can use it as a reminder when you have the opportunity to talk to someone.

Remembering the details of your history of abuse is an important step. If you don't know what the problem is, you can't solve it. To begin to solve the problems left from your childhood abuse, you must first remember the details of the abuse. Think about the feelings you have about the abuse. Recall any decisions that you made at the time. This sounds easy but is actually very hard. You probably have forgotten, repressed, or distorted much of your childhood. To remember an accurate picture of what occurred and how you felt is a slow process. Finding the truth about your abuse will require all your skills of remembering, thinking, analyzing, writing, and talking to get it into perspective. Even after you have worked long and hard on your past, expect to occasionally be surprised by new memories.

Start from the Beginning

As you remember your childhood, try to think of all the ways that you were abused. An example of the most common form of childhood abuse that many men overlook is abuse secondary to your parents' alcohol or drug problems. Child abuse that occurs as a result of your parents' use of mind-altering substances may not look like abuse until you think about it. Parents or guardians who spend too much of the family money on drugs or alcohol, often leave their families deprived of food, medical care, clothes, and even shelter. (This is neglect and is a form of abuse.) Many alcoholic or addicted parents lose control of their anger or frustration and hit, beat, or severely punish their families. (This is often physical or emotional abuse.) It is not unusual for a parent to be drunk or on drugs when they sexually molest one of their children. At the very least, an alcoholic or addicted parent is often a poor role model, may be neglectful, and have poor parenting skills. These parents frequently lack consistency in their guidance and may play "mind games" with their children, a form of mental abuse. Substance abuse can clearly be an instrument of childhood abuse. Consider Fred's experience:

> Fred's mother was an alcoholic. She was often drunk and left the care of his two younger brothers and sisters to Fred. Though Fred was only a ten-year-old and inexperienced, she would beat him if he made a mistake. In much of Fred's life he was afraid to try anything new for fear of making a mistake and being punished.

As you go through your history consider the part that alcohol, drugs, mental illness, gambling, sex, anger, or so- called religious practices may have had in your abuse. As you remember your abuse, don't allow yourself to be overwhelmed with rage. Occasionally, men want to get even as they remember their past abuse. Be patient. Look at how you are feeling. Ask yourself if these feelings are similar to the feelings at the time of the abuse. What did you do with the feelings in the past? Be sure to remember negative, socially deviant ways that you may have acted as a teenager or adult. It is common for you as a sexual offender to remember the details of how badly you were abused by your parents, but to forget the details of how you have abused your parents, wife, or children. Keeping in mind the extent of your own failure often is an aid to learning forgiveness for others. Forgiveness helps you let go of the anger toward others you have held on to for a good part of your life.

How Did Abuse Affect You?

The next step in your recovery is to consider the effects that the abuse may have had on you. In essence, some of the major effects of abuse are that it erodes trust, creates fear, destroys discipline, demolishes self-esteem, and creates selfish thinking because the abused person thinks that they must survive by "looking out for #1." Alcoholism and drug addiction again provide very common examples to show the effects of abuse. These addictions often result in dysfunctional families, personal degradation, and general failure. If you were brought up in an alcoholic home (or suffered other abuse) you may have been affected in the following ways:

1. Because you have low self- esteem, you may be an overly serious person who finds it difficult to have fun. You take everything too seriously.

2. Because of low self-esteem you think that you can never do a good job. Therefore, you may have a difficult time following through on projects or other ambitions.

3. Because you have little trust, you may be very hard on yourself. You may judge yourself harshly and not allow the time, patience, or flexibility that you need to succeed.

4. Because of low-self esteem, you may find yourself wondering if you are normal or not. At the very least, you may see yourself as different from others and use this as an excuse to act differently.

5. Because you are selfish, you may lie to get what you want. You may begin to believe your own lies. You may or may not be able to keep up with the lies that you tell.

6. Because you are suspicious, you may have a difficult time forming close relationships with others, especially with people of the opposite sex.

7. Because of suspicion and lack of confidence, you may experience a variety of sexual problems.

8. Because you are suspicious, you may have problems trusting others.

9. Because you are suspicious and lack confidence, you may find yourself feeling unsafe or vulnerable around others.

10. Because you lack confidence, you may find yourself constantly seeking approval and acceptance from others.

11. Because you are selfish and suspicious, you may find yourself angry much of the time and over-react to situations and events.

12. Because you are selfish, you may find that you are irresponsible in most, if not all, areas of your life.

13. Because your role models used drugs or alcohol, you may find that you too resort to the use of drugs and alcohol. You use them in an attempt to cope with everyday life stress.

14. Because you lack discipline, you may find that you are either compulsive, impulsive, or both.

15. Because you lack discipline and are selfish, you may frequently feel confused and frustrated.

16. Because you are suspicious and lack self- esteem, you may be a loner who withdraws from others frequently.

17. Because you are selfish and undisciplined, you may find that you do not responsibly manage your financial affairs.

18. Because of your lack of trust and confidence, you may discover that you seek out destructive relationships with others. Your relationships are based on dependency or other unhealthy attractions.

19. Because of your selfishness and suspicion, you may find yourself incapable of loving others.

20. Because of your selfishness and lack of self-esteem, you take unfair advantage of others and become abusive.

21. Because of your lack of confidence, trust, and discipline, you are a shallow and immature individual.

22. Because of your suspicion and selfishness, you may find yourself constantly in conflict.

23. Because of all of the above, you may feel like you are out of control of your life. You feel helpless and, at times, may even feel as if you are going insane.

These long-term effects of an alcoholic or drug-abusing family, are similar to the effects of other forms of abuse and neglect. If there was sexual abuse, then these effects may have been even more severe. These are just a few of the many effects of abuse. If you were raised in a dysfunctional family, you have experienced many of these effects. You may have experienced other more horrible results that you attribute to the effects of your abuse.

What Do You Do Now?

Part of dealing with abuse is learning to accept that it happened. The above list may be helpful to you in understanding some of the issues in your life that you may have as a result of your abuse. Understanding what the issues and problems are, is an important step toward resolving them. You can heal yourself from the effects of an abusive past, many people do. But you must choose to work at it.

As you learn more about abuse, you may discover that you have been denying how it has affected your life. Denial is a relatively common experience among victims of abuse. Denial means to pretend that something did not happen or did not affect you. It is usually the first way people react to abuse (and other forms of violence too). If you do it often enough, denial can later become a way of life. Denial is often a way of hiding feelings and thoughts that are very painful to recall. Consider John's case:

> John was abused. His father sexually molested him for five years. Part of the time when his father was fondling him, John enjoyed it. The sexuality felt good, but afterwards, he felt disgusted and hated it. He hated himself because he was participating over and over again in what he regarded as a degrading situation. Because he was a child, he was unable to stop his adult uncle when he also began molesting him. John felt powerless about his life. He feared that he would become a homosexual as a result of his abuse.
>
> Finally, John ran away from home to get away from the abuse. He decided that no one was ever going to make him look bad or weak again. He began to fight if anyone put him down. He left jobs if he wasn't given what he thought he deserved. He tried to overpower everyone who came into contact with him. All the while he would say to himself, "I'm tough. No one has ever taken advantage of me."
>
> When he was finally arrested and was forced to admit that he had big problems, he reluctantly came to therapy. At first he denied the possibility that he had ever been weak or not in charge of his life. Later he began to admit that for years he had been a powerless victim while he was abused. Still later, he realized that all his life he had been trying desperately to be powerful and in control so he would not be revictimized. Only when his denial broke down could he talk about his abuse. He then began to learn healthy and appropriate ways not to be victimized.

John later learned that, like many other victims, he had built an emotional wall around himself. He realized that he did it to keep distant from others so he would not experience more emotional pain or disappointment than he already had. This wall or shield is often referred to as emotional insulation. If you have been abused, you probably have a lot of insulation that keeps you isolated. It will take work to get free of it. Remembering details, sharing them with friends, and having the courage to do some hard work are some of the requirements for freeing yourself from the effects of abuse.

Chapter Eight Assignments

• Do Not Write In This Workbook •

If you have been the victim of abuse, you may find the following assignments helpful in understanding negative patterns about yourself and working towards recovery.

20 Think about your goals for being in treatment. What kinds of emotional insulation do you carry that keeps people at a distance? How does this insulation affect you as you try to reach your goals? Is your emotional insulation related to your own abuse? If so, how?

21 In this assignment, follow steps 1 through 6 to look at positive and negative qualities in yourself and others.

1. Make a list of the qualities that you like in other people.
2. List reasons why you think these qualities are important.
3. Now make a list of qualities you dislike in others.
4. Again, write down on this list reasons as to why you do not like these qualities in other people.
5. Now make a list of the qualities you would like to have for yourself.
6. Identify why you think that those qualities are important to you.

22 A part of getting healthy is looking closely and honestly at yourself, then working to change those things about yourself that you don't like. Are there qualities on your list that you don't like in others that you see in yourself? Look at your reasons for not liking those qualities. Once you are aware of the qualities that you want to have, you can slowly work at changing the bad qualities by replacing them with the listed qualities you desire.

Review your answers to these assignments with your therapist and your group. If you are working on your own, share your answers with a friend or person you trust.

CHAPTER NINE

Victims

Ultimately, there is one overriding reason for you to be in treatment. That is, you have harmed others, making them victims of your deviant behavior. Victims are also the final standard that must become very important in your future life. Having no more victims is also the measure of whether you are successful in your recovery or not. Even if you do not find satisfaction in your life, having no more victims means that you are in recovery. On the other hand, if you have more satisfying relationships, are successful in your career, and enjoy your life more but have even a single victim, then you have not made the slightest bit of real progress.

No matter how you feel as a sexual offender, you will never appreciate the full consequences of your deviant behavior on the victims. If, as a sexual offender, you are incarcerated and live a life behind bars for ten years, then you have paid a small price compared to what your victim will pay over a lifetime. The effects of abusive sexuality last long and go deep.

Victims may be emotionally or physically crippled. They may become totally impoverished. They may lose everyone they love as a result of a sexual crime. Nightmares, sleep disorders, sexual problems, uncontrollable anxiety, prostitution, eating disorders, lack of confidence, drug abuse, lack of self-esteem, hypochondria, alcoholism, confusion and an inability to make choices, guilt, depression, an inability to form lasting relationships, and self-defeating behaviors are some of the effects of sexual crimes on victims. In a good treatment program, you will learn the detailed effects of your crimes. If you are studying on your own, then you MUST read and think about the experiences that your victims have gone through and are now going through as a result of your crimes.

The final criteria of progress in therapy is not your level of satisfaction with yourself and your life. It is not how well you communicate. It is not your understanding. It is: **Have you changed your deviant ways of thinking, acting, and feeling? Can you and society be sure that you will never victimize any-one again?**

"Have you changed your deviant ways of thinking, acting, and feeling? Can you and society be sure that you will never victimize anyone again?"

Chapter Nine Assignments

• Do Not Write In This Workbook •

23 Think about your crimes. Consider what you did to the victims. Now, for the time during the first few hours after your crime:

1. List how you may have physically affected the victim(s).
2. List how you may have emotionally affected the victim(s).
3. List how you may have mentally affected the victim(s).

24 List how the victim's behavior may have changed in the months or years since your crime. Cover at least the following areas:

1. Sexuality
2. Friendships
3. Home life
4. Work or school
5. Close relationships (husband, parents, and so forth)
6. Trust
7. Finances (or parent's finances)
8. Self-confidence

Review your answers to these assignments with your therapist and your group. If you are working on your own, share your answers with a friend or person you trust.

CHAPTER TEN

Your Abusive Cycle

You have learned about common problems that affect many sexual offenders. You also learned that these problems are related to one another like the pieces of a jigsaw puzzle. You now know that committing a sexual crime is the result of a series of related steps that create a cycle of behavior. So, committing a sexual offense isn't the result of any one problem. It is the result of a cycle of erroneous thoughts, twisted feelings, and "sick" behaviors that you went through before committing a crime. Anytime you engage in criminal behavior, you go through a cycle of distorted thoughts, confused feelings, and abnormal behaviors. The whole chain of events is called an abusive cycle.

Until you look closely at your life, you probably are not aware of your abusive cycles. Discovering one's cycle of behavior takes time and requires that you take a close look at yourself and receive feedback from others about what they observe in you.

What Is Your Pre-assault Cycle?

To make it more easily understood, the abusive cycle is divided into two major parts: a pre-assault cycle and an assault cycle. A pre-assault cycle consists of a series of small behaviors, thoughts, and feelings that do not necessarily end up in criminal behaviors but often set the stage for the assault cycle to begin. For you and others around you, the components of the pre-assault cycle are an early warning system. They indicate that there is something wrong with how you are thinking, acting, or feeling about your life. If you want to avoid sliding into your assault cycle, you must identify the problem while it is still in the pre-assault cycle and correct it. The following are several common warning signs found in the pre-assault cycle:

1. Financial. You probably become irresponsible with money when you are not feeling good about yourself. As a result you begin to mismanage your money. This results in problems like not paying bills, spending money on drugs, writing bad checks, spending money foolishly, going on spending sprees, and misusing credit cards.

2. Employment. When you start having problems, you may begin to neglect your job, become very dissatisfied and switch jobs several times, or quit your job with no other options for work. You may become very angry at your employer and blame him for your dissatisfaction. It is common that you then use your dissatisfaction as an excuse to quit or to "get even." You may make excuses not to go to work, show up for work late, use drugs on the job, or lower your productivity significantly.

3. Social. You probably have some social problems during your pre-assault cycle. You probably have few friends and as you get closer to your offending behavior, you withdraw and isolate yourself even more. You might do this by consistently making up excuses not to go out with friends and avoiding new people. You may just stay at home alone for days, refusing to answer the phone or the door. You will probably begin to ignore family members, or get them to leave you alone by picking fights and arguing.

4. Education. If you are in school, then you may begin to take school work less seriously and end up with increasingly poor grades or drop out of school. You may skip classes, not do your homework assignments, or become bored and get angry at your teachers for not giving you what you think you deserve.

5. Drugs and Alcohol. You probably begin using alcohol or drugs. The use of these chemicals impairs your ability to think clearly and rationally and quiets your conscience. You may become more violent. If you have been using alcohol or drugs for a while, then your use increases. You may use daily (sometimes several times each day), spend needed money on drugs, have blackouts, start using alone, begin selling drugs, or become aggressive and obnoxious and provoke arguments.

6. Marital/Dating. If you are married or were living with someone, the chances are that this relationship began to have major problems before you committed your crime. You probably found excuses to be away from your partner. You may have had frequent fights and arguments. You might have begun putting your partner down in subtle ways. You began having serious sexual problems and may have started abusive sexual behaviors.

7. Leisure. Other warning signs that you are slipping into a pre-assault cycle involve leisure activities - what you do when you have nothing to do. It is likely that you have never developed appropriate leisure skills and activities.

Evidence of this would be not having any hobbies or interests that are important to you that do not involve abusive behavior. Activities such as excessive television watching, drinking or using drugs as recreations, driving aimlessly around in your car with no destination or purpose in mind, avoiding social activities with family or noncriminal friends, and not being willing to learn or take on new projects, hobbies, or interests all indicate problems with leisure time and are warning signs that you may be in a pre-assault cycle.

8. Health and Physical Appearance. When you begin to slide into an abusive cycle, you commonly let your health and appearance go down hill. You might not shave or bathe daily, you may dress sloppily or wear the same clothes for days, eat little or just eat junk food, and either lose or gain a lot of weight.

The above elements are common parts of many offenders' pre-assault cycles. You will need to look at your past life closely to see exactly how you act as you begin to behave in a deviant manner. Understanding this pre-assault cycle will be very important in learning how to intervene in your abusive behavior and will be an essential part of your overall recovery.

What Is Your Assault Cycle?

After the pre-assault cycle comes the assault cycle. All sex offenders have an assault cycle. It consists of several components:

1. The crime (often called an assault, molestation, or rape) you commit

2. The feelings that you have before the crime

3. The behaviors that you can observe yourself doing before the crime

4. The thoughts that accompany your feelings and actions

The Crime.

The crime is the abusive behavior you commit. For example, if you are a rapist, a description of your crime might read: "I rape adult women ages 19-35. I break into their houses late at night while they are sleeping and steal a knife from the kitchen. I go to their bedroom and place my hand over their mouth as I wake them up. I use the knife and threaten to harm them if they don't cooperate. I force them to perform oral sex on me and I force them to engage in anal intercourse." If you molest children, an explanation of your crime might read: "I sexually molest male children between the ages of 7 and 11. I usually meet a lone boy in the park. I lure him into the woods, telling him I know where there is a tree house. Once alone, I trick him into letting me suck his penis. I also have him masturbate me until I come. When we are through, I will give him two dollars so he won't tell anyone."

The Feelings.

The second component of an assault cycle is the feelings that you dwell upon as you near the offense. This may include such feelings as depression, anger, rejection, inadequacy, and many others. All of these negative states are vital for you to be in if you are going to commit a sexual crime. It is almost impossible to feel optimistic and enthusiastic about your life just before committing a sexual crime.

You will need to look carefully at your life to discover your behaviors in the assault cycle. Once you discover them, you will need to try to find the order of the behaviors so you can use them like a road map to tell you how close you are to an assault. When you see a danger sign, you can then intervene and stop your cycle from going further.

The Behaviors.

The next component is your behaviors. When you are drowning in negative feelings, you usually behave in ways that are easily observable. Examples of such behaviors are:

- ✓ Looking depressed
- ✓ Avoiding eye contact
- ✓ Becoming unusually quiet
- ✓ Pacing the floor, chewing fingernails
- ✓ Body becoming tense and rigid
- ✓ Becoming more secretive
- ✓ Grinning when extremely agitated or angry
- ✓ Covering up hurt or embarrassed feelings with laughter
- ✓ Face becoming red and splotchy, clenching fists
- ✓ Becoming sarcastic and argumentative
- ✓ Not answering when spoken to

- ✓ Distorting information
- ✓ Spacing out or staring vacantly
- ✓ Becoming overly passive or passive-aggressive
- ✓ Isolating and avoiding others
- ✓ Using drugs and alcohol
- ✓ Reading pornographic magazines
- ✓ Intimidating others
- ✓ Increasing use of profanity
- ✓ Increased stuttering
- ✓ Becoming sneaky and lying

The Thoughts.

The last component is the thoughts that you use to keep your assault cycle going. All sex offenders have cognitions or thought processes that are a part of their abusive cycle. You are no different. Many of the thoughts that keep the pre-assault cycle going are "errors in thinking." Below is a list of examples of the types of thoughts that often go through the minds of sexual criminals while in the assault cycle:

- ✓ I deserve sex.
- ✓ The more sex I get, the better I feel.
- ✓ I need sex as often as I want it.
- ✓ I feel inadequate to cope with my life.
- ✓ I feel insecure.
- ✓ I want to get revenge.
- ✓ People are purposely out to insult me.
- ✓ My friends are rejecting me.
- ✓ I shouldn't even try, I will fail anyway.
- ✓ At least I can enjoy my sexual fantasies.
- ✓ Women will never like me.
- ✓ Why is this happening to me?
- ✓ I'm never wrong.
- ✓ Everyone else is better than I am.
- ✓ If I play it right, I can get away with it.
- ✓ I won't get caught.
- ✓ I'm unlovable.
- ✓ I'm stupid.
- ✓ I'm a failure.
- ✓ I deserve to feel sorry for myself.
- ✓ People are no good.
- ✓ If it doesn't go my way, it's wrong.
- ✓ I'm the best. They're all idiots.
- ✓ If I'm a sex offender, why not enjoy it.
- ✓ My victims really liked what I did to them.

Defense Mechanisms

Thinking errors are an integral part of the abusive cycle. They are also called "defense mechanisms." Defense mechanisms are ways in which people avoid dealing with truth or reality. They enter into your committing a sexual crime by taking small steps. Like climbing the rungs of a ladder, each step up the ladder brings you closer to the point where you can overcome your moral awareness and commit a sexual crime. Common examples of defense mechanisms include rationalization, intellectualization, denial, minimization, and religiosity.

1. *Rationalization.* When you rationalize, you make excuses to explain and justify your behavior, even though you know that what you are doing is wrong. For example, "every woman likes to be *taken*" or "I was just educating her about sex."

2. *Intellectualization.* When you intellectualize something, you are avoiding reality by trying to explain away issues through abstraction or theorizing. You avoid dealing with real issues and emotions and try to make something sound OK even though it may be very abusive. For example, "I feel that every young girl should learn about sex from someone who loves and understands her" (as an excuse for molesting a six-year- old girl).

3. *Denial.* Denial is when you refuse to admit the truth about your crimes or the problems you have. Denial is very common among sex offenders. Denial, simply put, is not admitting the truth. "I never raped her" is an example.

4. *Minimization.* When you minimize your behavior, you try to make it out to be less serious than it really is. You intentionally downplay and understate the truth about a situation. "I only took her for a ride" (when discussing a kidnapping) or "I only touched her."

5. *Religiosity.* Many sex offenders become overly religious after they are caught. We encourage you to connect with a higher power and develop the spiritual side of your life. True spirituality supports your being responsible in your life. Religiosity is using your religion or spirituality to avoid being responsible. Some sex offenders use their religion wrongly. They try to make it an excuse to not involve themselves in treatment. They make statements such as "I am a Christian now and have to walk with God. I don't need treatment because I am saved and have been forgiven." This type of thinking tries to excuse you from personal responsibility by using religion inappropriately. Religion is not a crutch to avoid dealing with real life issues and problems, but is an aid and comfort to help you face reality.

Use your spirituality wisely so that your treatment will work with your religion and your religion will be supported by your treatment. If you find yourself in conflict or having a problem with your spirituality and treatment, consult with a clergy member or another person knowledgeable about both religious matters and sexual deviancy.

"Use your spirituality wisely so that your treatment will work with your religion and your religion will be supported by your treatment."

You have just read about some of the elements of the pre-assault and assault cycles. What you may not know is how all these parts fit together. Each step leads to the next one. The steps of the pre-assault cycle lead to the steps of the assault cycle. Each sex offender has his own unique cycle. Once you are in treatment, you will spend time exploring your cycles and developing cycle charts. The assignments at the end of this chapter will help you explore your pre-assault and assault cycles.

Chapter Ten Assignments

• Do Not Write In This Workbook •

25 Consider what "thinking defects" or defense mechanisms you have. Look in the material that you have read and you will find several. Make a list of your favorites. Give at least one example of how you use each of these thinking defects. Review your work in group. If you are working alone, review this list with a friend or friends who know you well.

26 Using the parts of pre-assault and assault/abusive cycles described in this chapter, make up a pre-assault and sexual assault cycle that describes your pattern of abusive sexual behavior. Be sure to include the thoughts, feelings, and behaviors that are part of each step of your cycle. In a well-done cycle there will be many steps. Try to describe at least seven steps that lead up to one of your assaults.

Review your answers to these assignments with your therapist and your group. If you are working on your own, share your answers with a friend or person you trust.

CHAPTER ELEVEN

Relapse Prevention: A Model For Change

A popular approach to helping sex offenders remain crime-free in society is **Relapse Prevention**. The techniques of relapse prevention have been used for years with sex offenders and for decades with alcoholics and drug abusers. If you learn to use relapse prevention skills consistently, they can be effective tools to avoid new sexual crimes.

The relapse prevention model suggests that there are no CURES for sexual deviancy. That is, no matter how strongly you feel that you will not commit another sexual crime, if you make the wrong choices and allow yourself to indulge in distorted thinking, feeling, and action, your sexual problems will return. However, it is possible to live a crime-free life by following the steps of the relapse prevention model.

The Potential to Reoffend

Contradictory as it may seem, the first and most important aspect of relapse prevention is the awareness of your potential to reoffend. Every sexual offender has the potential to reoffend. In fact, the reoffense rate of sexual offenders may be one of the highest of all criminal acts. The lowest estimates of men identified as sexual offenders who commit another crime is one man out of ten. The highest estimates suggest that as many as six out of ten men reoffend. If you have even one chance out of ten that you will reoffend, how important is that awareness? In any case, if you feel that you have no possibility of committing another crime, then you are much more likely to fall back slowly into the old behaviors that led you to commit a crime. Someone who denies his potential to reoffend is like an alcoholic who thinks, "I've handled my problem with alcohol." He then goes into a bar to see a friend. One thing leads to another and before long he is having "just a small one." For him, the first step toward not drinking again is to realize that he will always have the potential for a problem with alcohol and then to take preventive measures. Sexual abuse is much the same. The potential for future problems with sex is high. Therefore, you must learn "to be prepared." The relapse prevention approach will aid you in preparing to avoid future problems.

While you are involved with a treatment program or studying on your own, you will gain insights into your behavior. You will come to understand its causes and the tools you will have to use in order to avoid sexually abusive behavior. All of this information will be important. You have just learned something about cycles, defense mechanisms, the interrelationship of problems, and thinking errors. All of this information will be used as building blocks for developing a relapse prevention plan.

You Have Already Begun the First Step

The first step for relapse prevention is to become aware of the deviant cycle. You began gaining this awareness in Chapter Ten. There you learned that the abuse cycle is a series of steps that leads to a sexual assault. You learned that there are defense mechanisms you use to move your cycle from one step to another. In this chapter you will learn about another step of relapse prevention, high risk situations or events. These are situations, actions, or emotions that are signs to you that you are on the road to reoffending. They mean that you have started into your abusive cycle.

High Risk Situations

High risk situations or events come in a variety of forms. They may be external situations in your environment or they may be internal emotional states. An example of an internal risk situation might be when a strong emotion negatively affects how you feel and think. Often your reaction to stress is a risk situation. For example, when you have work or family problems, you may become tense and anxious. If you are tense, you may try to relieve your tension by masturbating to sexual fantasies. Another internal risk situation for many men is anger. Many offenders find that when they start getting angry they begin to think inappropriately. They start thinking "she owes me sex" or "it's not fair that they are getting good sex and I'm not." Obviously these types of thoughts and actions will increase the chances of sexually acting out and therefore are risk situations.

Risk situations may also be external. An activity or situation can make it easier for you to feel inappropriately aroused. For example, watching a pornographic movie could result in either a greater number of sexual fantasies or more deviant ideas about sex. Another example of the kind of external risk situation that men with problems sexualizing boys put themselves in would be for them to decide to go for a walk and "just happen" to walk by the video arcade where attractive teenage boys hang out. Still another example of an external risk situation that applies to a rapist is his driving around aimlessly. When he does so he is more likely to see potential victims. The following example illustrates a high risk situation. It uses an example of successively higher risk situations for drinking alcohol. Many men have problems with alcohol, so this example may help you better understand risk situations. The same principle applies to sexual abuse.

> Bob has a history of alcohol abuse and has been diagnosed as an alcoholic. He went through a treatment program for alcoholics and stopped drinking. He has been sober for six months. Bob no longer drinks but often does not know what to do with his time. Today he is lonely and bored. He goes out for a walk when he bumps into Joe, an old friend and drinking buddy. Bob is lonely and is glad to meet Joe even though he remembers that one of Joe's favorite activities is to drink. Bob knows that Joe will use every opportunity to do so. They meet on the street and talk for a while. When Joe asks Bob if he would like to sit down somewhere so they can talk more comfortably, Bob says sure. Without saying where they are going, Joe then leads the way to the Watering Hole Tavern. When they arrive Bob knows he shouldn't go in, but decides not to tell Joe about his drinking problem. Bob is embarrassed and doesn't want Joe to think he is weak. Instead he says to himself, "I will just say no." They go in and Joe sits down and tells the bartender to bring him a drink. He remembers Bob's favorite drink and, without asking Bob, orders it for him. Bob then is in a bind. He may refuse Joe's friendly offer and possibly offend him, or drink it. So he say's to himself, "Well, I'll have just one." Several hours later Bob leaves the bar, drunk and broke again.

What Could Bob Have Done?

There are several things Bob did in this situation that he should not have. Before you read on, try to find at least six poor decisions Bob made. Write them down on a piece of paper before reading on. Now, read on, comparing your list to the points below.

First, when Bob finished treatment, he should have filled the gaps in his life that were left when he stopped drinking. He had to find new, healthy activities. Just stopping drinking (or sexual abuse) is not enough. You often have a hollow empty feeling and wonder what to do with it. All the time and energy that was directed towards alcohol (or sexuality) must be redirected into healthy activities.

Second, Bob should have tried to keep the conversation with Joe brief. Sometimes you have to give up old friends when you go through treatment. Often these "friends" are a dangerous attachment to the past and a very negative influence. Bob knew from his past experiences with Joe that Joe would probably look for an opportunity to sit down and have a drink. He could have told Joe that he was late for an appointment and had to run, thereby cutting the conversation short.

Third, instead of being assertive and suggesting a safe place to go, like a coffee shop, Bob passively followed Joe. He did not think. If he had, he would have remembered that Joe would probably want to drink.

Fourth, Bob should not have been embarrassed to tell Joe that he doesn't drink alcohol any more. By being direct and honest, Bob would have kept himself out of trouble and may have even helped Joe.

Fifth, when Bob saw where Joe was leading him, he could have not gone in. Not drinking is easier when not in a bar. By the time that Bob was sitting at the bar with a drink in front of him, it would have taken superhuman effort not to drink.

Sixth, no matter what the pressure, Bob should have never taken the first drink. It made no difference where he was, what the circumstances were, how embarrassed he felt, or what pressure Joe put on him. For Bob, the first drink and the last are not far apart.

These six points are examples of behaviors that are high risk for someone with Bob's problem. You, with a history of sexual deviance, also have high risk situations that make it easier for you to make bad decisions. For example, consider the problems of a child molester named Dean:

Dean is on probation for sexually abusing two boys, ages nine and ten. Part of his probation is to complete a treatment program for sexual offenders. Dean has been in treatment for several months. During this time he has not sexually acted out, but he is lonely and not interested in doing much. One day Dean decides to visit a woman acquaintance. When he gets to her house, he discovers that she has a new roommate, Joan. Joan now lives there with her children, a five-year-old girl and a nine-year-old boy. Being lonely, Dean accepts his friend's invitation to come in and have some coffee. Joan is talking about her new car and how great it drives. After a while she turns to Dean and asks him if he will watch the kids for "just a moment," while they go for a test drive. Dean, trying to please her, says yes. Soon he is alone in the house with the two children. As he hears the women drive off, the children come to investigate him. He smiles at them and says hello. The next thing that he knows, the children are jumping on the couch next to him and asking him to read them a story. Dean picks up the book, puts his arms around the kids, and begins reading.

Now, Dean is in the same position as the recovering alcoholic who is sitting at a bar. It is very easy for him to take the next step and reoffend. There are several poor decisions that Dean made as he placed himself in a high risk situation. Take a moment before reading on to list them on a piece of paper.

What Could Dean Have Done?

The following are some of the ways that Dean put himself into risk situations:

First, when Dean discovered there were children in the house, he should have excused himself. He could have told his friend that he would come back to visit her later when she wasn't so busy.

Second, when the women went outside, Dean should have followed them outside instead of staying indoors with the children.

Third, when the women began to leave Dean alone with the children, he should have said "no" and told his friend that he needed to go.

Fourth, Dean should never have allowed himself to be alone on the couch with two children.

The Essence of Relapse Prevention

There are two main ideas behind relapse prevention. First, with care and hard work you can anticipate risk situations and avoid them. The second idea is that you can have escape plans laid out. If you recognize that you are in a risk situation, then you can immediately get out of it. If you don't, then you may begin to get into trouble or the risk may get greater. It is inevitable that from time to time you will find yourself in a risk situation. When you do, as you can see from the examples above, there are opportunities at every step of the way to intervene and remove yourself from the high risk situation before you reoffend. If you do not intervene, then the risk of a reoffense becomes greater.

Consider Dean's case. He was in no risk when he was following his treatment plan. As soon as he entered a house where two adult women were watching the children, his risk increased. When he entered the house, it made it easier for the next step to happen. When he ended up alone with the children, he found himself in even greater risk. Compare this to Bob's case. Bob was not at risk of drinking when talking to a friend on the street, but doing so made it easier for him to take the next unhealthy step-going into a bar.

Recognizing that you are in a risk situation gives you time to use the tools you have learned. With quick intervention, correcting the problem is relatively easy to do. The longer you wait, the more risky the situation will become and the harder it may be to get out of it. Dean could easily have said "no" before going into the house. Bob could have said "let's go for coffee" before Joe led him to the bar.

Another aspect of being in risk situations is that they can fool you. The first time you are in a risk situation and do not intervene may not cause you any problem. But after the second or third time, you will start to get more comfortable and forget that it is a risk situation. So, when you start to get into trouble, it will take you by surprise. Also, the more times you are in a risk situation, the harder it is to get out of it. In Dean's case, he had not molested the children up to the point of reading the story. If he continued to sit with the children, or began to think that being alone with children was not a risk, then the chances are greater that he will eventually molest more children.

Are You in a Risk Situation?

How do you recognize that you are in a risk situation? First, you must know all the aspects of your abusive cycle. Then you must identify the specific situations that in the past have started you off on abusive behaviors. Next, you must become aware of the thoughts, feelings, and behaviors that you use to allow yourself to stay in the risk situation. There are limitless numbers of examples of each. Below are a few examples:

Risk Situations:

(These are often unique for each individual.)

✓ Visiting beaches

✓ Baby sitting

✓ Aimless driving or cruising

✓ Hanging around and watching women or children in parks

✓ Going into pornography shops

✓ Visiting friends who think about sex in abusive ways

Thoughts:

(These are what you think to make it OK to stay in a risk situation.)

✓ I can handle it.

✓ It doesn't really matter if I'm here.

✓ No one cares about whether I stay.

✓ I'm a failure so why bother trying.
✓ I'm no good so I may as well enjoy it.
✓ I'm not strong so you can't expect me to...

Feelings:

(These are often the excuses that give power to the thoughts.)

✓ Feeling depressed
✓ Feeling angry
✓ Feeling confused
✓ Feeling bored
✓ Feeling anxious
✓ Feeling frustrated
✓ Feeling lonely
✓ Feeling fearful

Behaviors:

(These are often the excuses that give power to the thoughts.)

✓ Having sexually abusive fantasies
✓ Using Drugs
✓ Isolating yourself from others
✓ Going to bars
✓ Looking for victims
✓ Neglecting your responsibilities
✓ Arguing and/or fighting

These examples illustrate the ways most sex offenders set themselves up to reoffend. They begin to ignore the warning signs or red flags and then use deviant thoughts and behaviors to make the situation worse. Figure #6 on the next page illustrates these principles.

A Simple Tool That Always Works

Relapse prevention involves not only awareness but also requires that you have certain tools that you can use to intervene. Sometimes interventions are very simple, such as using avoidance to prevent yourself from getting into a high risk situation. A basic avoidance tactic for child molesters might be to look the other way or cross the street when they see children. For rapists, an avoidance tactic might be not to go driving aimlessly with no purpose or destination in mind. In other cases, a sex offender might need to use stronger intervention, for example, calling a friend or therapist if he begins having abusive sexual thoughts or fantasies.

The diagram proposes that: (1) relapse is a process occurring over time, not a sudden and complete failure resulting from a single yes or no choice; (2) while a person may make several decisions leading him closer to reoffending (or maintaining abstinence), the opportunity to progressively change one's direction always exists; (3) each choice is important in that it approaches abstinence or relapse more closely; and (4) most sexual offenders will fall in the middle of the diagram (neither in total control nor totally out of control). The decisions printed in upper- case (capitals) indicate the treatment route you must take not to reoffend (continued abstinence). The decisions printed in lower-case letters indicate behaviors or feelings that are warning signs that you are getting off the healthy track into a high risk situation and closer to reoffense (relapse). Your goal is to learn to recognize when you are on the track to a new crime (relapse) so you can intervene immediately.

Every sexual offender, if he is honest with himself, experiences times when he begins to slide into his cycle of abusive behaviors. You are no different. These occurrences will happen to you from time to time. The goal is not to panic or give up, but rather recognize that you are putting yourself in danger of committing another crime and intervene immediately. If you do this consistently, you will avoid getting into serious trouble. The key is self-understanding and self-awareness allied with good behavior.

There is a lot for you to learn about relapse prevention. As you become more involved in treatment you will hear more about this and begin to learn how to make these tools work in your daily life. It may seem to be a lot of work right now, but as you begin to practice the new skills you learn in treatment, these principles become natural and are easier to use.

Figure #6

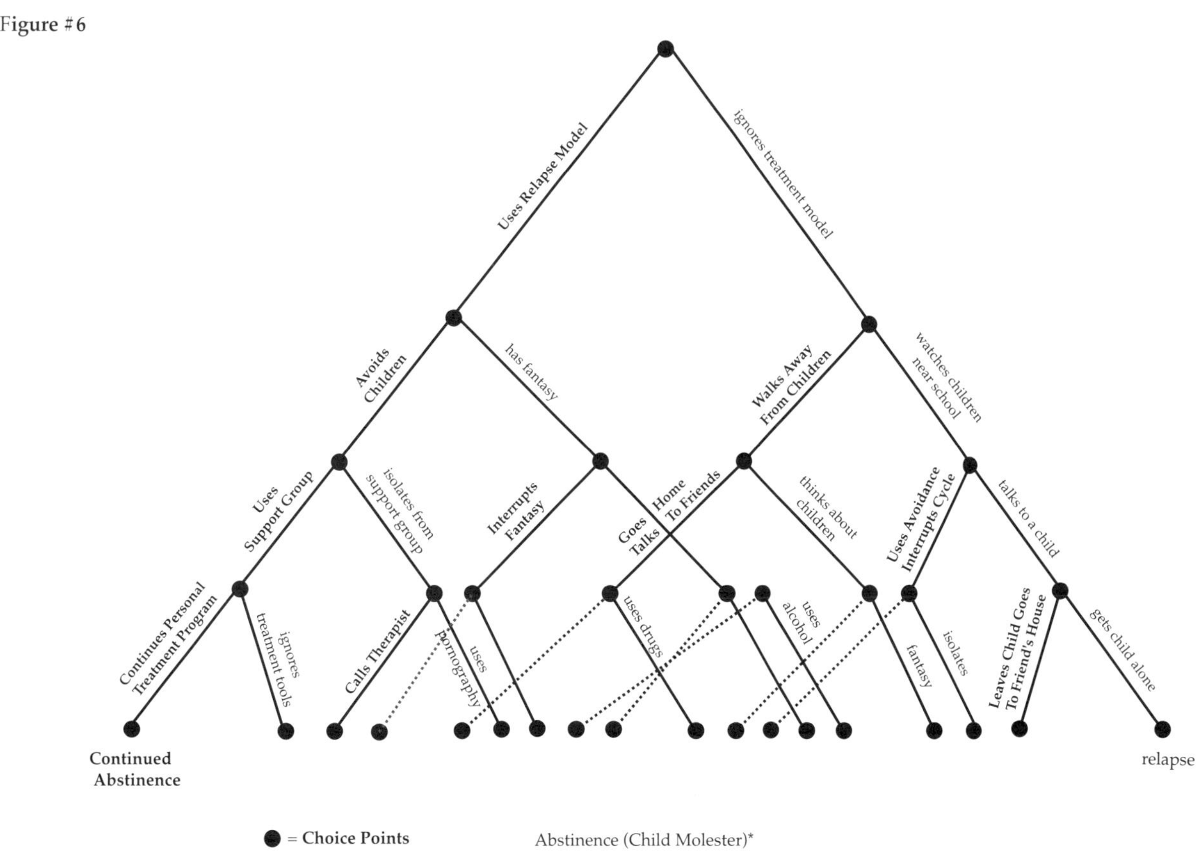

Abstinence (Child Molester)*

Chapter Eleven Assignments

• Do Not Write In This Workbook •

27 Make a list of the behaviors, places, thoughts, and emotions that, based on your past behavior, indicate that you are at a higher risk to reoffend. Share this list with your group and therapist. If you are working alone, review this with a friend or friends who can give you feedback.

28 Go back to Assignment #27. For each item you identified, write down at least one intervention that you could use. An intervention means a way of stopping yourself so that you do not increase your risk to reoffend. Share these interventions with your group, therapist, or friend(s). Interventions that you can use may include avoidance of the situation, escaping from or leaving a threatening situation, or other coping responses such as talking to yourself to stop a behavior, talking with a good friend about your problems, and so forth.

Review your answers to these assignments with your therapist and your group. If you are working on your own, share your answers with a friend or person you trust.

CHAPTER TWELVE

The Stages of Recovery

By now you have read most of this manual and done many of the assignments. If you have been in a treatment program, you have probably been in group therapy as well. If you are working on your own, you have had a lot of time to dwell on the topics in this workbook. Your work has already influenced you somewhat. As you go further, you will find that you will go through several general stages as you move towards recovery. You won't go through these stages once and leave them behind forever. They tend to cycle over and over. You will find that you deal with issues from stage one, move on to work on issues from later stages, and then find yourself facing your first issue again. This is normal. You will notice though, that each time you work on an issue it becomes easier to handle and you will work through it more quickly. Success is not like climbing straight up the side of a mountain where you see the scenery once, and then it is behind you. It is more like climbing the mountain by going around it. With each circle you make, you find yourself back at the starting point, only higher. When you circle enough, you reach the top.

<u>The Stages</u>

Stage One: Anxiety and Suspicion.

Therapy is a scary new idea. At the beginning of your recovery from sexual deviancy, you are apt to feel suspicion and apprehension. This is most likely true if you have joined a treatment group. Often it is worst when you first walk into the room with other offenders. If you are reading this book alone, you probably questioned if it had anything in it that was really worth reading. This reaction is normal. The task for you in the beginning is to keep reading or attending. Try to keep an open mind and be patient. You will soon become more comfortable and be ready for Stage Two.

Stage Two: Optimism and Hope.

By this time you have done some reading, met some of the other men, and gotten an overview of therapy. It is typical at this stage for you to feel optimism and hope. Often, starting to get comfortable, learning about what is ahead in therapy, and speaking openly to other men without rejection will give you a positive feeling that you are in the right place and everything will work out all right. This is an easy stage and one that you will return to many times as you continue in therapy. Your task at this stage is to make the most of it. Dig deep into your mind, get honest, do your homework, and share your insights. The caution is not to expect too much return at first. Even when you are feeling good about your work, don't expect others to jump up and down at the same time. Just do your work. Take the feedback you get and go on.

Stage Three: The Struggle to Go On.

This stage occurs when your initial enthusiasm begins to wear off. It is often accompanied by a feeling of restlessness or boredom. The excitement of a new program is gone. You know the ropes and you feel that there is not much to which you can look forward. This is a critical stage of therapy. It is often the stage in which most men who enter treatment begin to fail. This is because when you start getting bored, what was easy at first now becomes hard work. If you try to avoid hard work, then it is easy to become very critical, seeing all the shortcomings of therapy, and eventually talking yourself into quitting. Your task at this stage is to learn to keep your eye on your goal and work steadily towards it. This is the time to use all the help that you can get from reading or friends.

Stage Four: Solid Progress.

This stage is the most important stage. Getting through Stage Three successfully is hard, but getting through it shows that you really are changing. If you are working solidly, then this is the stage where you get some real rewards. The reward that you get is not money, freedom, or pleasure. It is power, power over yourself, your emotions, and your thoughts. It means that you have begun to develop the part of your personality that can help you to achieve goals and live a satisfying life. At this stage, your work may be interesting or not, but you know that you can do it without collapsing into anger and fear. You may feel depressed or excited but you know that you can keep on working regardless of which feeling is present. It is a powerful state.

Common Experiences in Recovery

While you are working on specific issues, there will be other emotional patterns that you experience. These patterns are often a series of specific emotions that are common reactions to working on a specific issue. Often these emotions will be part of a cycle that goes on inside the four major steps first outlined. Working with your history of abuse is a good way to understand what you may encounter as you progress.

Confusion

If you have started to remember your childhood abuse, you may first experience confusion. This is especially true if your abuser was a parent, guardian, or someone close to you that you trusted. When people you know and trust hurt you and misuse the trust you place in them, confusion is a common reaction. Often this is because you trusted them and were harmed because of your trust. You may also have flashbacks, bad dreams, and thoughts about the abuse, all of which add to your confusion. Confusion sets in because you get conflicting information and can't tell which to believe.

Anger

The next phase or reaction you may experience is anger. Most people who were abused feel angry at the person who was the abuser, anger at themselves, or both. Your anger may be a result of the suffering you have experienced. In part, it may be because of the frustration of having no way to release the fear, anger, and pain. You may have released your anger in an unhealthy way and gotten into greater trouble because of it. This not only adds to the anger but to the confusion as well.

Minimizing

A common way of reacting to anger and frustration you may have experienced because of abuse would be to minimize the abuse. You may have told yourself things like, "It wasn't all that bad," "It doesn't happen all that often," "He or she had a good reason for doing it," or "I deserve what happened to me." If your abuser was someone you know, loved, or trusted (such as a parent), you may have minimized the abuse because you were protective of this person at the same time you were feeling angry. Because the awful truth hurts terribly, it is very common for people to be protective of those who are important to them. One way to be protective and not face the truth about abuse is to minimize the behavior of others who have harmed you.

Cloudy Memory

Another common experience as you try to resolve the problems that your abuse may have caused you, is to find that your memory is sketchy. That is, when you try to remember, you find that your memory is cloudy and vague. You don't remember much of what happened during your abuse. You may remember that something happened or you may remember a few details, but you can't seem to get the big picture. This selective memory process can often be overcome if you try to do so. It requires a step-by-step effort to clear the clouds of years of denial. Try to recall the events one at a time. For example, if you were beaten, try to remember each instance and gradually the big picture will emerge. Slowly, let the memories come out and talk about them. Talking about them is a way to enlarge on your recall. Each memory, when you pay attention to it and recall it fully, will lead to other memories. Lastly, accept the fact that the memories may be painful. If you ask for support, you can cope with them. Remember that you are not alone.

Destructive Roles

Another reaction to remembering your abuse is the awareness that you have developed specific "sick" roles or ineffective behaviors. Often these roles are developed as a means of protecting yourself and learning how to survive. As you become aware of your abuse, you also become intensely aware of the amount of hard work that you have to do to overcome the long-term effects of your abuse. This awareness is sometimes overwhelming and you may feel discouraged at this point. There is no need. Sometimes this work, though hard, can be very exciting and liberating. So keep looking and remembering.

In addition to the stages of recovery, often there are some old roles that need to be changed. The following are some examples of roles that you might find as you investigate your abuse:

Loner

A typical pattern that you might discover is that you became a "lost child," or a "loner." Often you feel worthless, so you try to hide from people and try very hard NOT to be noticed. You may think and tell yourself, "Once a victim, always a victim. Who would want me? Nothing matters. No one cares." Your self-esteem is very low and you avoid dealing with others at all costs. Often this pattern leads to great loneliness and then to abusive behavior as a way of getting attention.

Tough Guy

A second role that sexual offenders often find, is that of the "tough guy" or the "martyr." This role results in the individual portraying an image of "Nothing or no one can hurt me!" If you are this type of person, you may do everything you can to hide your fear and anxiety. You may pretend that you can go anywhere, fight anybody, or take any punishment. You then have to numb the pain from these behaviors in any way you can. The over use of drugs and alcohol is a common method of numbing this pain. Your tough guy image is also a way in which you find you can keep others at a distance and not allow them to get close to you.

The Time Bomb

A third role that is common for sexual offenders to play is a pattern of "acting out." These people are sometime called "walking time bombs." They carry around all of their pain, frustration, fear, and anger and are ready to "explode" at any time. The slightest problem, event, or provocation can result in their acting out in some way against themselves or others. If you discover that you have developed this role you are probably angry most of the time. You find yourself looking for arguments or fights so that you have an excuse to blow up and vent your rage.

The chances are that as you work on your history of childhood abuse, you will be overwhelmed when you realize that you have developed one or more roles like these. These roles were the ways that you originally learned to cope with the world around you and your inner life. Nonetheless, they have to be changed. As they are, none of these old roles are going to help you feel better. They are often old reactions to abuse. If you continue to react to your life in old blind ways, you will never feel better.

In order to begin understanding what has happened to you, why you have been the way you are, and what you can do about it, you need to get beyond the old reactions to your abuse. You must enter a new phase of recovery.

Recovery

The relief begins to come after you have worked hard on your problems. It is a sign that you are beginning to recover. Recovery is, simply put, leaving old "sick" ways of being and starting to live a new healthy life. As you begin to resolve your problems, you will get to a point where the abuse no longer affects you as seriously as it has in the past. Reaching this point requires you to use all the steps shown in this manual. Recovery results in your learning to control your life, instead of letting life's events control you. As you recover, you will have a greater understanding of your thoughts and feelings. Recovery demands that you build trust, even as you take risks to help yourself.

Lastly, though this chapter has focused on your abuse, remember that your victim or victims are going to have to experience the same horrible consequences. You may have damaged many productive lives by your sexual deviancy. In treatment you will spend many hours trying to learn to empathize with your victims' pain. One step in this process is to remember your own.

The assignments at the end of this chapter are some basic steps you can take in order to help yourself into recovery. Reading other self-help books will further assist you in working with the abuse and your own recovery.

Chapter Twelve Assignments

• Do Not Write In This Workbook •

29 After identifying negative beliefs, you can begin to establish new positive beliefs about yourself by using the following procedure:

1. Sit in a comfortable place and relax.
2. Close your eyes and imagine a white screen in your mind.
3. Allow a negative belief to come into your emptied mind. For example, if you are used to telling yourself that you are a failure, allow that thought to come into your mind.
4. Now STOP that thought. Some ways to stop thoughts might be: to try saying "stop" in your mind; to make your mind blank; or to replace the negative thought with a positive one. (If you need help finding positive thoughts to replace your negative ones, look at the list of positive factors you generated in Assignments #5 & #8.)
5. Continue practicing this thought-stopping exercise under these ideal conditions.
6. Later, try to stop these thoughts while you are going about your daily tasks.
7. Begin to keep a daily log of your experiences.

Review your answers to these assignments with your therapist and your group. If you are working on your own, share your answers with a friend or person you trust.

Congratulations on working through this book!
You have made a good start on your treatment. Remember that one book or a few treatment sessions are not a cure for sexual offending. It will take more information, learning, practice, time and work to change your life so that you will have no more victims.

There are additional workbooks in the Paths To Wellness set of workbooks for sexual abusers. *Why Did I Do It Again* helps you discover and examine in detail all the steps in your sexual abuse cycle, and *How Can I Stop* will help you develop the tools you need to intervene in your sexual abuse cycle and prevent yourself from reoffending. *Enhancing Empathy,* teaches you about empathy a skill you need to develop so that you will have no more victims and will be able to build a better social life. Another book that will be useful to you is *Men & Anger: Understanding and Managing Your Anger*. It uses the relapse prevention skills you will learn from these workbooks to help you with the problems you have with destructive anger outbursts. Finally, *Paths to Wellness* will help you look at personal recovery for a variety of problems using a holistic/integrated approach. You may order these books through NEARI Press, or they may be available through a treatment program, library, or book store. Good luck, and keep your personal treatment and recovery program going!

NEARI PRESS TITLES

The NEARI Press
New England Adolescent Research Institute
70 North Summer Street
Holyoke, MA 01040
Phone (413) 540-0712

Forthcoming! 2005. **Current Perspectives: Working with Sexually Aggressive Youth and Youth with Sexual Behavior Problems** by R. E. Longo & D. S. Prescott (Editors). NEARI Press. **ISBN# 1-929657-26-9**

Enhancing Empathy by Robert E. Longo and Laren Bays (1999). NEARI Press. Paperback, 77 pages. **ISBN#1-929657-04-8**

Growing Beyond by Susan L. Robinson (2002). NEARI Press. Paperback, 216 pages. **ISBN# 1-929657-17-X**

Growing Beyond Treatment Manual by Susan L. Robinson (2002). NEARI Press. Paperback, 42 pages. **ISBN# 1-929657-15-3**

Lessons from the Lion's Den: Therapeutic Management of Children in Psychiatric Hospitals and Treatment Centers by Nancy S. Cotton, Ph.D. (2005). NEARI Press. Paperback, 354 pages. **ISBN# 1-929657-24-2**

Men & Anger: Understanding and Managing Your Anger by Murray Cullen and Robert E. Longo (1999). NEARI Press. Paperback, 125 pages. **ISBN#1-929657-00-5**

Moving Beyond Sexually Abusive Behavior: A Relapse Prevention Curriculum by Thomas F. Leversee (2002). NEARI Press. Paperback, 88 pages. **ISBN# 1-929657-16-1**

Moving Beyond Student Manual by Thomas F. Leversee (2002). NEARI Press. Paperback, 52 pages. **ISBN# 1-929657-18-8**

New Hope For Youth: Experiential Exercises for Children & Adolescents by Robert E. Longo & Deborah P. Longo (2003). NEARI Press. Paperback,150 pages. **ISBN# 1-929657-20-X**

Paths To Wellness by Robert E. Longo (2001). NEARI Press. Paperback, 144 pages. **ISBN#1-929657-13-7**

Power Struggles: A Book of Strategies for Adults Who Live and Work with Angry Kids. by Penny Cuninggam (2003). NEARI Press. Paperback, 112 pages. **ISBN# 1-929657- 23-4**

Respecting Residential Work With Children by James R. Harris (2003). NEARI Press. Hardcover, 163 pages. **ISBN# 1-929657-21-8**

Strong at the Broken Places: Building Resiliency in Survivors of Trauma (2005).by Linda T. Sanford. NEARI Press. Paperback, 208 pages. **ISBN# 1-929657-25-0**

The Safe Workbook for Youth by John McCarthy and Kathy MacDonald (2001). NEARI Press. Paperback, 210 pages. **ISBN# 1-929657-14-5**

Who Am I and Why Am I In Treatment by Robert E. Longo with Laren Bays (2000). NEARI Press. Paperback, 85 pages. **ISBN#1-929657-01-3**

Why Did I Do It Again & How Can I Stop? by Robert E. Longo with Laren Bays (1999). NEARI Press. Paperback, 192 pages. **ISBN#1-929657-11-0**

Using Conscience as a Guide: Enhancing Sex Offender Treatment in the Moral Doamin by Niki Delson (2003). NEARI Press. Paperback, 102 pages. **ISBN# 1-929657-22-6**

Using Conscience as a Guide: Student Manual by Niki Delson (2003). NEARI Press. Paperback, 50 pages. **ISBN# 1-929657-28-5**

~ ~

For prices and shipping information, or to order, please call:
Whitman Distribution 800.353.3730

Find us on line at: www.neari.com

NOTES:

NOTES: